THE U.S. SPACE PROGRAM AFTER *CHALLENGER*

THE U.S. SPACE PROGRAM AFTER CHALLENGER

WHERE ARE WE GOING?

ALAN STERN

A GROLIER COMPANY

FRANKLIN WATTS
NEW YORK/LONDON/TORONTO/SYDNEY/1987
AN IMPACT BOOK

Frontispiece: the space shuttle *Atlantis* roars into orbit.

All photographs courtesy of NASA except the following:
UPI/Bettmann Newsphotos: p. 44; University of Colorado: pp. 73, 110;
Eagle Engineering, Houston, Texas: p. 121.

Library of Congress Cataloging-in-Publication Data

Stern, Alan.
The U.S. space program after Challenger.

(An Impact book)
Bibliography: p.
Includes index.
Summary: Discusses the investigation into the
Challenger catastrophe, the reshaping of NASA, the
debate over manned versus unmanned space flights,
and the future possibilities for commercial
enterprises in space.
1. Astronautics—United States—Juvenile
literature. 2. Challenger (Spacecraft)—Accidents—
Juvenile literature. [1. Astronautics.
2. Challenger (Spacecraft)] I. Title. II. Title:
US space program after Challenger. III. Title:
United States space program after Challenger.
TL793.S74 1987   387.8'0973   87-14765
ISBN 0-531-10412-5

C O N T E N T S

ACKNOWLEDGMENTS

The preparation and presentation of this book could not have been possible without the help of many friends. First on my list are, of course, Lou Hall and Tim Schaffner, who encouraged me throughout, and Maury Solomon, who provided warm and invaluable guidance from the outset.

To those specialists who took the time to read and critique chapters, I owe a special gratitude; their insights and careful criticisms vastly improved the manuscript.

Thus, a special thanks to Charles Barth, Kent Tobiska, Dave Siskind, Jeff Hoffguard, Don Hearth, Paula Gay-Fagre, Richard Fagre, Larry Esposito, Kim Chantala, Bill and Cheryl Dennler, and again, Lou Hall. Heather Hollingsworth's keen editorial eyes and patient pen also merit heartfelt thanks.

For motivation I owe a personal thanks to Ron McNair, who will never know the impression he left on my career.

Finally, I thank my Carole, who read every word—twice—and who is fast becoming an expert in space history (like it or not!). Again, bashfully last on my list, but first in my heart.

FOR FIVE FLIERS,
FOUR OF THEM BABY BOOMERS,
THREE OF THEM SCIENTISTS,
TWO OF THEM PILOTS,
(EACH OF THEM VIBRANT)
EVERY ONE OF THEM GONE.
—*Ad Astra Per Aspera*

TO MY GRANDFATHER
AND MY GRANDMOTHER

P R E F A C E

The space program has changed a great deal since the destruction of the space shuttle *Challenger*. The nation's perception of NASA and the U.S. space program have changed as well.

The purpose of this book is to examine the future of the space program in light of the *Challenger* disaster. We begin by reviewing the history of the space program, for in its history are the motivations and lessons that may guide its future. Next, in Chapter Two, the *Challenger* accident is described, as are the official findings about its cause. In Chapters Three through Seven, a series of issues fundamental to the space program's future are discussed, including the uses of people in space and the future of space commercialization. The high cost of space exploration is also reviewed, and measures to reduce these costs are explored. Finally, in Chapter Eight, we examine the alternative future paths the space program could take.

Throughout the text, we will be pursuing the answers to two important questions: Has anything good come of the *Challenger* disaster, and has the shuttle accident forced the space program to improve?

Challenger *lifts off from its launch pad*
on January 28, 1986, at 11:38 a.m., Eastern
Standard Time. Seventy-three seconds later,
the vehicle would explode, killing its crew of seven
and destroying the multibillion-dollar craft.

C H A P T E R
O N E

HISTORICAL
PERSPECTIVE

ONE FINE DAY

It was a fine day—clear and cold—with the kind of sky pilots call "the blue bowl." At NASA's Kennedy Space Center in Florida the space shuttle was poised for another mission. The temperature stood at 38° Fahrenheit.

NASA, the space shuttle *Challenger*, and its crew of seven stood ready to launch the twenty-fifth flight of the shuttle program. The pace of events quickened as the launch neared. First, the shuttle's flight computers were loaded with their programs for launch. Then, the final loading of the fuel tanks was completed. Aboard *Challenger*, the seated astronauts checked their controls. On schedule, less than five minutes before launch, huge internal turbines were started to produce the power needed to activate *Challenger*'s control systems and steer its engines. With the shuttle ready for flight, the launch team retracted the wiring umbilicals and fluid lines to the craft and turned full control of the countdown over to the onboard computers.

At exactly 11:38:00 A.M. *Challenger*'s engines ignited, and the 4.5-million-pound (2-million-kg) craft began the familiar climb into orbit. Within seconds, the 180-foot-long (56-m) shuttle had cleared the launch tower and had turned along its planned flight path. *Challenger* then accelerated, speeding through Mach 1 (the speed of sound) in about forty seconds. All appeared to be going well, and the crew's commander reported this to Mission Control.

Then, while still accelerating, *Challenger* suddenly exploded, disintegrating into thousands of twisted shards and a great fireball thousands of feet across. It was exactly seventy-three seconds into the flight.

The explosion that destroyed *Challenger* (NASA's second and most experienced space shuttle) also destroyed the two satellites carried in its hull. The shuttle's crew, consisting of Commander Francis (Dick) Scobee, Pilot Michael Smith, Mission Specialists Ellison Onizuka, Judith Resnik, and Ronald McNair, Payload Specialist Gregory Jarvis, and Space Flight Participant (Teacher-Observer) Christa McAuliffe were killed.

In the days that followed the *Challenger* disaster the nation mourned. President Reagan eulogized the crew both in a nationally televised speech and at a memorial ceremony at NASA's Johnson Space Center in Houston, Texas. People across the country wept, recalling similar national tragedies such as the sinking of the *Titanic* in 1912 and the assassination of President Kennedy in 1963. After the accident came a wholesale evaluation of the space program's merits, its goals, and its purposes.

In the wake of the *Challenger* disaster and the investigation into its cause, a whole series of issues concerning our nation's future in space came to the fore. In this book, we will examine these issues. We will ask why certain things happened and what changes can be made to prevent them from happening again. We will explore possibilities and examine alternatives. We will see that space policy issues affect our nation's entire economy and technology base and that these issues are rather complex. But before examining the pivotal choices facing the United States in space, we must first review what led us to the present situation.

THE SOVIET *SPUTNIKS*

The Space Age began on October 4, 1957, with the launching of the world's first satellite, *Sputnik 1.* Chilling headlines announced the Russian launch to a stunned America. The Soviet satellite was a technical coup. Previously, the Soviet Union had been viewed as a sluggish and backward giant, battered by World War II, struggling even to feed her own people. Almost overnight, *Sputnik* changed the world's image of the Soviet Union.

To scientists around the world, *Sputnik* represented the opening of a new frontier. From earth orbit satellites could be used to improve communications, routinely monitor weather patterns, and study the earth and heavens as never before.

To engineers, *Sputnik* represented a technical achievement of stunning significance. Although the United States had been planning to launch a satellite of its own, the device (called *Vanguard*) would weigh only a few pounds. Sputnik weighed almost 200 pounds (90 kg)! The implications were clear—the Soviets were able to build very large rockets and complex guidance systems. Clearly, the USSR was not the backward giant Americans had believed.

Among politicians and citizens alike *Sputnik* created a crisis in confidence about our standing as a world leader. Although the Eisenhower White House announced that "we have never thought of our program as in a race with the Soviets,"[1] Army General

James Gavin said that the Russian satellite represented a "technological Pearl Harbor."[2] In 1957, the Japanese surprise attack on Pearl Harbor was barely sixteen years in the past, and Gavin's analogy struck an important chord in the American psyche. Then-Senator Lyndon B. Johnson said, "I for one don't want to sleep under the light of a Soviet moon." British writer C.P. Snow said the United States had been jolted from its "technological conceit."[3]

In response to Sputnik's launch, efforts to loft the American satellite Vanguard were redoubled. Plans were set for a December launch. However, even before Vanguard could be fully prepared, the Soviet Union launched Sputnik II. The new satellite weighed 1,120 pounds (504 kg) and carried complex experiments, including a life-support system and a live dog! Sputnik III would weigh over 3,000 pounds (1,364 kg).

Suddenly, Vanguard's 3-pound (1.4-kg) cargo seemed almost embarrassing. The Senate opened an investigation. This inquiry was led by Lyndon Johnson, who would later both recommend the Apollo program to President John F. Kennedy and then carry it out during his own term as president.

Once Sputnik II was in orbit, then-Soviet Premier Nikita Khrushchev made it clear that his rockets, although intended for peaceful purposes, could also be used to send nuclear weapons across the globe quickly. This kind of speechmaking, backed up by the orbiting symbols of Soviet technological superiority, brought space into the realm of serious politics.

In the United States, plans were made for a series of larger booster rockets and more satellites. Meanwhile, tiny Vanguard was readied for flight.

During the early years of the 1950s, military and scientific research had been carried out on brief rocket flights into and above the atmosphere. Additionally, the army had set about developing "ballistic missiles," such as the Redstone and the Atlas. These missiles were designed to carry nuclear bombs through space to targets around the world.

Taking advantage of the missile technology, a plan was formulated in 1955 by the White House and the scientific community to launch a series of small research satellites. These small spacecraft were to be launched in 1958 as part of the International Geophysical Year (IGY) research effort. The project was named "Vanguard." When the Soviet Union announced its intent to also launch a satellite during the IGY, the United States barely noticed.

The surprise 1957 launching of *Sputnik I*, followed quickly by the much larger *Sputnik II*, changed many things. The *Sputniks* became a symbol of national embarrassment, and space exploration became a major national goal. In schools, new science and math education programs were introduced, homework was increased, and students were counseled to take engineering and science majors in college. In industry, aerospace and propulsion engineers, computer technicians, and scientists of all kinds were suddenly thrust into high gear. Dr. Thomas Kronke, a space engineer and former air force officer who entered high school in 1957, has said, "It was as if our parents realized their generation had been sleeping on the job and sent us out to solve the problem."[4]

By December 6, *Vanguard* was ready to go. American politicians boasted in the days before the launch that our satellite program, though small, was superior because it was conducted in public, for all the world to see. And the world did see. *Vanguard* lifted off on live television, rose less than a foot, then crashed back to the ground in a ball of flame.

With this defeat, the stakes rose again, and calls were made to form a space agency within the government. Inquiries were held to determine the technical reasons why *Vanguard* had failed. Investigators found more wrong than bad design. Poor management and inadequate planning were found to be root causes behind the technical problems.

Meanwhile, President Dwight D. Eisenhower gave the U.S. Army the go-ahead to launch a small satellite weighing some 18 pounds (8.1 kg) on a missile called the Jupiter-C. The Jupiter-C had previously been banned from space missions because it was developed as a weapon, and President Eisenhower wanted a civilian cast to the U.S. effort. However, given the embarrassing failure of the *Vanguard*, the president relented. The Jupiter-C project was led by German rocket pioneer Wernher von Braun, an accomplished engineer and space visionary. At one point in 1956 von Braun had considered launching a satellite during a Jupiter-C test flight but had been specifically ordered not to by the White House. As 1957 turned into 1958, in quiet secrecy the Jupiter-C and its satellite, *Explorer I*, were prepared for flight.

By January 31, 1958, all was ready and the rocket was launched. Within ninety minutes, tracking stations in the western United States confirmed that *Explorer I* was in orbit. We, too, now had a satellite!

THE FORMATION OF NASA

The explosion of the *Vanguard* vehicle in December 1957, and the continuing Russian launches in the months that followed, provided compelling reasons to form some kind of U.S. space agency. In the spring of 1958, legislation was introduced into Congress to form the National Aeronautics and Space Administration (NASA). The National Aeronautics and Space Act constituting NASA was signed into law on July 29, 1958, and the new agency opened its doors for business on October 1, 1958, just sixty days later.

NASA was formed out of an older government research agency called the National Advisory Committee for Aeronautics (NACA). NACA had been conducting high-speed aircraft research, including research on the famed X-15 supersonic airplanes.

NASA's program was set up quickly under the pressure of increasing Russian spectaculars. NASA's first administrator, Dr. T. Keith Glennan, set up temporary offices in Washington, D.C.'s Dolley Madison House. Rumors spread of an impending Soviet manned flight.

The 1958 Space Act specifically set out several purposes for the new agency. Included in these were continued aeronautics research, the exploration of space, and the development of manned spaceflight. From NACA, NASA inherited some 8,000 employees and five research centers, such as the Langley Research Center in Norfolk, Virginia. NASA also absorbed the California Institute of Technology's Jet Propulsion Laboratory (JPL), which had built the Explorer I satellite, and von Braun's rocket team at the Army Ballistic Missile Agency in Huntsville, Alabama. In 1960, the Huntsville site was renamed the George C. Marshall Space Flight Center.

Among the programs NASA started in its early months were the Explorer scientific satellite series, the Tiros weather satellite series, the "man-in-space" Mercury program, and a new large rocket program known as Saturn. Among the engineers NASA inherited from JPL, Huntsville, and NACA were men such as Max Faget, Chris Kraft, Bob Gilruth, and Hugh Dryden, each of whom would later play an important role in the Apollo and shuttle programs.

Thus, at its very inception, NASA was given the people and technological resources to undertake large and complex research programs. The money needed to build and support NASA and its projects also flowed freely in the early years after Sputnik. The nation had decided that it was going to be a power in space, and NASA was charged with carrying out that decision.

THE EARLY YEARS

The years from 1959 to 1966 can be considered the height of the space race. It was during these years that the United States and the Soviet Union vigorously competed for prestige and technical accomplishments in space. Toward the end of this period, countries such as Canada, India, Britain, France, and Germany also began to operate satellites and rockets.

In 1959, both the United States and the Soviet Union began to accelerate the rate of satellite launches, and a Soviet satellite weighing over 5 tons was orbited. Work also began on manned satellites. The Soviet man-in-space program was called *Vostok* (meaning "East"), the NASA project, as said earlier, was called Mercury. In both programs, the key goal was to determine if humans could withstand the rigors of launch and landing and to see if the body's systems could survive weightlessness.

During the early years of the Space Age, the Soviet Union held its lead. Each year the Soviets launched more and heavier satellites than did the United States. This capability was a direct result of the emphasis the Soviets had placed on rocket research during the 1950s. Russia used this enormous advantage to score a great number of "firsts" in space. In their unmanned program, the Soviets achieved the first spaceflight of animals (1957), sent the first probes into solar orbit (1959), obtained the first photographs of the far side of the moon (1959), made the first launch of a probe to Mars (1961), and completed the first landing of a spacecraft on the moon (1966). With their manned programs, still more firsts were achieved, including the first man in space (1961), the first man to spend a day in space (1961), the first woman in space (1963), the first multiman crew in space (1964), and the first walk in space (1965). To underscore their achievements, the Soviets reminded the world that "cosmonette" Valentina Tereshkova accumulated more time in space than did all of the Mercury astronauts combined. For a time it seemed as if the Soviets could accomplish anything they wished to in space and that their spectacular achievements were carefully planned to upstage whatever accomplishments the United States could muster.

Still, NASA was gaining ground fast. Having started with a severe lack of launch capability, the United States concentrated on three broad fronts: developing larger rockets, conducting a wide variety of research projects, and learning how people could be useful in space. Many of the U.S. gains were the direct result of electronics miniaturization, which allowed engineers to package more sophisticated systems into the small satellites NASA rockets could launch.

KENNEDY CALLS
FOR BOLDNESS

President Kennedy, who was elected to succeed Eisenhower in 1960, was an ardent supporter of the space program; so was his successor, Lyndon Johnson. Kennedy watched Soviet space triumphs repeatedly upstage American gains during 1961, his first year in office. This string of successes culminated on April 12, when the Soviets put Major Yuri Gagarin into earth orbit.

Seeing the Soviet successes as a challenge, President Kennedy directed Vice President Johnson to determine how the United States could catch up. In forming a group to assess U.S. space goals, Kennedy

Mercury was America's first manned spaceflight program. In this picture, John Glenn is being launched aboard the one-person Mercury-Atlas 8 spacecraft to become the first American in orbit.

President John F. Kennedy was a strong supporter of space exploration. In 1961 he directed NASA to "land a man on the moon" before the end of the 1960s. His dream was realized in 1969.

asked, "Is there any place we can catch them? What can we do? Can we leapfrog them?"

Shortly after Gagarin's flight, the first American was launched into space on a 15-minute suborbital hop along the Atlantic coast off Florida; the astronaut was Lt. Commander Alan B. Shepard, Jr. Three weeks later, fresh from this success, Kennedy decided to set a manned lunar landing as a national goal. The lunar-landing effort came to be known as Project Apollo. At its peak, Project Apollo involved hundreds of thousands of people and required the development of whole new technologies, including huge launch vehicles larger than anything the Soviet Union had (or to this date has) developed. When Kennedy announced this goal, he said, "We choose to go to the moon and do these other things not because they are easy but because they are hard. . . . No single space project in this period will be as exciting, or more important to mankind . . . and none will be so difficult and expensive to accomplish."[5]

Kennedy's speech invigorated Congress and the public. NASA was set in high gear; it was authorized to catch up with and surpass the Soviets, whatever the cost.

In the months following Kennedy's announcement, the Apollo project took shape. Included in the moon-landing effort were a series of unmanned reconnaissance probes to the moon, known as *Ranger, Surveyor,* and *Lunar Orbiter.* Each of these was designed to scout out certain scientific information required to design the Apollo spacecraft. Additionally, a new manned space project known as Gemini was conceived. The *Gemini* spacecraft, which was to carry two men into orbit, was designed to test the complex rendezvous and docking techniques required for Apollo. The Gemini program would also be used to demonstrate that people could walk in space, and that periods of weightlessness of up to a week (which were required for the moon trip) would not be harmful. The Apollo effort also included the development of a series of powerful new rockets, known as the Saturn series.

MERCURY, GEMINI, AND OTHER SUCCESSES: NASA GAINS MOMENTUM

In 1962, NASA put the first American in orbit, Colonel John Glenn. Later, three more astronauts rode *Mercury* capsules into orbit, the last of which flew for thirty-four hours. Also in 1962, the United States sent the unmanned probe *Mariner 2* to Venus. In 1963, the first prototype large Saturn rockets were launched. In 1964, NASA orbited the first weather satellite, *Tiros*. *Tiros* proved that spacecraft could do useful work in addition to research. In 1965, NASA opened its new manned spacecraft center in Houston, Texas. Today this facility, which contains the space shuttle's Mission Control, is known as the Johnson Space Center. Also in 1965, the *Ranger* probes photographed the moon from close range, and the first high-altitude satellites were launched to improve telephone and TV communications. Later that same year, the first five *Gemini* flights were launched, and *Mariner 4* reached Mars. In 1966, the first *Surveyor* lunar lander was launched to test lunar theories and certain technologies for Apollo. *Surveyor* succeeded on its first try! In November of that year, the Gemini program came to a close after ten flights, and NASA announced that Apollo launches would begin in 1967—less than six months away.

THE APOLLO PROGRAM

It was hoped that manned flight tests on the Apollo project would start in early 1967, with the launch of

Apollo 1. Following that flight, a series of up to ten increasingly complex missions were planned to test the Saturn boosters and the *Apollo* and lunar module spacecraft. Additionally, these flights would serve to explore space between the earth and moon and to provide experience in manned lunar orbit operations. Unfortunately, this elaborate plan was never carried out.

About a month before its planned launch, on January 27, 1967, the *Apollo 1* spacecraft caught fire during a ground test. Three astronauts were trapped aboard; they perished in less than a minute. Across the country people were stunned. President Johnson received word of the tragedy at the signing ceremonies of the first U.S./Soviet International Space Treaty. Following the fire, a commission was set up to investigate the cause and recommend improvements to the spacecraft's design. Senate and House hearings were also held to examine the root causes of the mishap. The commission's findings, and those of the Congress, pointed in similar directions. The *Apollo* spacecraft had many design flaws, and slipshod workmanship was evident throughout the program. Additionally, poor management techniques and a lack of adequate quality control were cited as contributing factors.

While NASA set about an eighteen-month redesign and test program to alleviate these problems, some in Congress called for abandonment of the lunar-landing goal. Critics argued that the space program was an "obscene" waste of money at a time when poverty, hunger, and other social concerns required more funding. Space program detractors also noted that the Soviets hardly seemed to be in a race with us to the moon. Overall, public support waned dramatically during 1967 and 1968, and NASA underwent a series of severe budget cutbacks.

The Apollo program finally got flying in October of 1968 with *Apollo 7*. This earth-orbital flight was a complete success and led to an ambitious plan to launch *Apollo 8* on a bold lunar-orbit mission. *Apollo 8* was launched on December 21, 1968. Its successful flight around the moon made Kennedy's 1969 target date for a landing once again seem possible. In addition to its technical achievements, *Apollo 8* included a stirring and memorable live television reading of the Bible from lunar orbit that Christmas Eve. The space program was back in high gear.

Apollo 9 and *Apollo 10* flew in early 1969; these missions tested the lunar module—*Apollo*'s landing craft. Then, on July 16, 1969, *Apollo 11* roared off its launch pad at the Kennedy Space Center. Three days later, astronauts Neil Armstrong and Edwin (Buzz) Aldrin, Jr., landed their craft on the moon. Astronaut Michael Collins circled overhead in the *Apollo* mothership. On July 20, 1969, Armstrong stepped onto the dusty lunar plains and proclaimed, "That's one small step for a man, one giant leap for mankind."[6] The country broke out in unabashed pride, and congratulations poured in from around the world. President Richard M. Nixon traveled to the South Pacific to greet the crew on its return and hailed the period as, "the greatest week in the history of the world since the Creation."[7]

Above: A three-man Apollo spacecraft orbits the moon. This picture was taken from the Lunar Module landing craft returning from its moon base. Below: Twelve Apollo astronauts landed on the moon. During moon walks, astronauts set out experiments, took pictures, and collected soil and rock samples for study on earth.

THE SOVIETS RETREAT FROM
THE MOON BUT ACCELERATE
EARTH-ORBITAL WORK

What had the Russians done since their early successes? How had the United States succeeded in reaching the moon first?

On the unmanned front, the Soviets were conducting a vigorous program of scientific research, military intelligence gathering, and rocket development. They were operating three launch sites in different parts of their country by the mid-sixties and were launching over sixty payloads per year. Their manned program, however, waned. In 1966, they conducted no flights at all as they prepared a new craft, called *Soyuz* (meaning "Union"), which was comparable to *Apollo*. However, the first flight of *Soyuz* (in June 1967) ended in tragedy as the craft plummeted to the earth and the cosmonaut was killed.

Like NASA after the *Apollo 1* fire, the Soviets took more than a year to resume manned flights. After they did, however, their large moon rocket (the *G-1*) exploded during ground tests. Left without a means of getting their craft to the moon, the Soviets quietly withdrew, denying there had ever been a race or that they had ever intended to send anyone to the moon. In place of a manned lunar program, they instead launched a series of unmanned lunar rovers and sample-return missions, which they boasted were a much cheaper way of studying the moon than was manned exploration. Shortly thereafter, the Soviet manned program was redirected to focus on long earth-orbital flights and space station activities.

AFTER APOLLO:
A SMALLER NASA

Almost as soon as *Apollo 11* completed its mission, renewed calls were made to further cut back the space program. Some cutbacks had taken place as early as 1966, when public opinion first began to change. At that time, NASA Administrator James E. Webb was told by President Johnson that Vietnam and other priorities had replaced NASA in the budget. Webb argued that the United States should follow Apollo with other ambitious goals but was rebuffed. He resigned in 1968 and was replaced by Thomas Paine, his deputy. Shortly thereafter, Senator Edward Kennedy (the late president's brother) called for a slowdown of the space program, and Congress cut the 1969 NASA budget back to its 1963 level. In this cutback three *Apollo* landings were canceled, the upcoming *Skylab* program was cut in half, unmanned missions to Mars were delayed, and all plans for post-Apollo lunar exploration were abandoned. Military space programs, including a manned orbital laboratory, were also dropped.

As the Apollo program finished up, making five additional successful landings on the moon, some of which included a lunar rover and advanced scientific exploration gear, the Nixon Administration called for an assessment of the United States's future goals in space. This assessment was made by a select committee known as the Space Task Group (STG), which was headed by then-Vice President Spiro Agnew. Agnew was a vocal supporter of the space program and recommended a lunar base, a landing on Mars in 1980 or 1986, and a space station in earth orbit, but his plan fell on deaf ears. NASA itself, under Administrator Paine, then recommended a program focusing on more practical benefits. Paine asked for a space station and a space shuttle, as well as continued unmanned exploration of the planets leading perhaps to a manned Mars effort by the year 2000.

Although Paine's plan for NASA's future was more closely aligned with the nation's expressed desires than was the Agnew/STG report, it, too, failed to gain support in Congress. As a result, many space projects were canceled or scaled back. NASA floundered for direction. By 1973, NASA's funding had dropped to barely half the level it was in 1968. As dollars were squeezed, *Apollo 18* and *Apollo 19* were canceled, as was a second *Skylab*. NASA's Space Telescope project was also set back, as were efforts to place landers on Venus and roving explorers on Mars. The early 1970s were a difficult time for the space program. NASA's government and contractor work force dropped from over 350,000 to less than 140,000. Many engineers, technicians, and scientists who had worked to put *Apollo* on the moon lost their jobs. Historians, such as Professor John Logsdon of George Washington University, have analyzed this period and concluded that concerns over social issues, ecology, and an "anti-technology" backlash in the wake of the Vietnam War were major factors in NASA's decline.

A NEW ADMINISTRATOR, A WORKABLE COMPROMISE

In time, Administrator Paine left NASA for private industry, and the agency got a new boss, Dr. James C. Fletcher. Dr. Fletcher was a former university president with close ties to the academic community. At his Senate confirmation hearings, Fletcher said he hoped he could bring a strong scientific focus to the space agency. Fletcher also stated that he was determined to mold a compromise between NASA's engineers and scientists and the Congress, so that the space program could "get on with its future."

Early in 1972, after months of intense negotiations, Fletcher gained approval in the Nixon White House and in Congress for a scaled-down space shuttle program and a series of unmanned explorations of the earth's environment. However, plans for a space station, continued lunar exploration, and the Mars mission were sacrificed. Although many space enthusiasts felt the "Nixon-Fletcher deal" was not sufficiently challenging, it did ensure a continued manned presence in space—a presence that had been jeopardized.

The space shuttle was a project NASA had dreamed of undertaking since the agency's inception. Its inclusion in Fletcher's compromise was a victory for NASA. The shuttle (as it later became known) was to introduce the era of reusable, rather than expendable (throwaway), launch vehicles. By reusing the same craft again and again, it was reasoned, the costs of space exploration would be drastically reduced. The proposed shuttle would also make possible satellite repair, the re-outfitting of satellites for second missions, the construction of very large stations in orbit, and the routine transport into space of the most useful tool of all—people.

Fletcher was happy with the compromise he worked out because he believed that the shuttle was the key to many other projects NASA wanted to eventually undertake. Engineering studies had proven that without the shuttle, the space station and the Mars mission would prove impossible to carry out. Fletcher hoped that once the shuttle was flying, NASA's other ambitious projects would quickly get underway.

ANOTHER DECADE

Despite budget cutbacks, the decade of the 1970s was a busy one for the space program. This was primarily due to the leftover momentum given it in the 1960s. However, we will see that the rate of new activity slowed each year in the 1970s.

NASA's unmanned space efforts of the 1970s were

diverse. A series of large and small astronomical observatories were launched to study the universe; these satellites (with names such as *Uhuru*, *Copernicus*, and *Einstein*) revolutionized the science of astronomy by observing the death of stars, the heart of the galaxy, and objects as old as the universe itself, among other phenomena. Unmanned probes were also sent to the planets. In 1972, *Mariner 9* mapped Mars, and in 1976 two *Viking* landers made the first studies of the Red Planet from its surface. *Viking* discovered many things about the composition of Mars and conditions on the Red Planet but failed to find convincing evidence of life. Also in the seventies, *Pioneer 10* and *Pioneer 11* each explored Jupiter, and *Pioneer 11* went on to Saturn. Additionally, the *Voyager* probes were launched in 1977 on a decade-long exploration, which is still continuing, of the outer solar system. Studies of the earth were also expanded, as a series of crop and mineral resource survey satellites known as *Landsat* were launched. Two new generations of weather satellites were also launched in the seventies, and weather forecasting from space became routine. A clear focus of NASA's work was the return of tangible benefits from space. This emphasis grew largely out of the redirection of the space program after Apollo.

Manned programs continued in the 1970s but at a much reduced pace. After the last *Apollo* landed on the moon in 1972, the *Skylab* minispace station was launched. During three visits to the *Skylab* orbital workshop, American astronauts spent months at a time exploring the sun, the earth, and the effects of weightlessness on the body. Carried out with leftover Apollo program hardware, *Skylab* was a huge success. To NASA's disappointment, however, *Skylab* was not immediately followed up by a permanent manned space station.

*Skylab was home to nine U.S.
astronauts in 1973 and 1974.*

In assessing the knowledge gained during *Skylab*, NASA has said that the greatest findings were not scientific but operational. Foremost among the touted benefits from *Skylab* were the lessons learned about the uses of people in space. *Skylab* astronauts demonstrated that humans could greatly improve upon robot observations made from space, primarily by being on the spot to make changes in plans when necessary. Additionally, *Skylab* astronauts demonstrated that people could repair complex systems in space. On one occasion such repairs saved the space station from certain failure.

After *Skylab*, only one other manned spaceflight was carried out by the United States during the 1970s. This was the 1975 Apollo-Soyuz Test Project. This mission concentrated on joint experiments by American and Russian astronauts during a three-day linkup in space. Although this flight was largely an exercise in U.S./Soviet diplomacy, it did teach NASA a great deal about the workings of the Soviet space program.

For manned and unmanned missions alike, NASA had little success in obtaining permission to start new projects in the 1970s. Although a hundred satellite projects were started in the 1960s, the 1970s saw only about twenty-five. No manned projects except the shuttle were started. By the mid-1980s, such cutbacks would leave the American civilian space program almost without any new projects at all.

Outside NASA, however, the pace of activities quickened. Military satellites performing reconnaissance tasks became a cornerstone of arms treaty verification, and numerous communications satellites were launched for business and industry. In Europe, a consortium (grouping) of over sixteen nations formed the European Space Agency (ESA) to explore and exploit space.

The Soviets themselves carried out a vigorous space program in the seventies. In many ways it paralleled the U.S. scientific exploration and unmanned weather and earth-resources programs. Soviet probes repeatedly landed on Venus, and attempts were made to land on Mars (though none succeeded). As it had in the early sixties, the Soviet program greatly surpassed the U.S. effort. Their manned program, for example, carried out twenty-six flights (to our eight), which concentrated on building space stations, launching some six *Skylab*-like *Salyut* stations. Although the Salyut missions were usually successful, two had to be aborted due to technical failures. Also, in 1971, a returning three-man space crew was killed during re-entry when a hatch seal blew and cabin pressure was lost. Still, the Soviets pressed on, perfecting techniques such as automatic docking in orbit (which NASA has still not attempted) and conducting manned missions lasting as long as six months.

THE DEVELOPMENT OF
THE SPACE SHUTTLE

The space shuttle program had two major goals at its outset. These were 1) to develop the world's first reusable spacecraft, and 2) to make space transportation less costly and more routine. These goals were interrelated, since reusability was associated with lower costs.

From a technical standpoint, the shuttle was designed to carry up to seven people and 65,000 pounds (29,000 kg) into earth orbit. According to plan, the shuttle would be capable of carrying not just career astronauts but also scientists and even non-scientists. By opening up spaceflight to many more people, NASA believed greater benefits would accrue. Mission durations of up to thirty days were originally planned, so that the vehicle could act as a minilaboratory in orbit.

As it was first envisioned, the space shuttle was to be capable of making up to sixty flights per year. Also, the shuttle was planned to eventually operate at a profit, so that NASA and taxpayers could recoup the $5.2 billion that had been required to finance its development. Prospective shuttle users included the scientific community, the military, and commercial industries as diverse as communications, pharmaceuticals, and oil.

The shuttle's design featured three major components: a winged "orbiter," in which the crew would live and work, a huge external tank (ET) to hold the fuel required for ascent into orbit, and twin solid rocket boosters (SRBs) to help power the initial launch phase. Although original plans had envisioned a fully reusable system, including a manned booster (as opposed to the solid rockets), a partially reusable design was adopted for development. This "hybrid" design was selected because it was less expensive to develop. Thus, the shuttle that was actually built included an orbiter that could be reused up to a hundred times, solid rocket boosters that could be reused perhaps ten times, and an external tank that could not be reused. Although this hybrid design saved on development costs, it proved to be much more expensive to operate than a fully reusable shuttle would have been.

On the launch pad the combined vehicle would stand 184 feet (56 m) tall and would weigh some 4.5 million pounds (2 million kg). The orbiter itself would be 121 feet (37 m) long and weigh as much as an airliner. Compared to the 11-foot (5-m) tall *Apollo* capsule, the reusable shuttle was an ambitious undertaking.

When the shuttle program officially began in 1972, three major aerospace firms were hired to build the vehicle's major components. Rockwell International built the airplane-like orbiter; Martin Marietta built the huge external fuel tank; and Morton Thiokol built the twin solid rocket boosters used in the early portion of each launch.

The final design chosen by NASA and its aerospace contractors was supposed to permit the shuttle to take off without the week-long countdowns common to Apollo, fly in orbit with a minimum of ground control, and land on a runway. These attributes were incorporated to allow airline-like operations and a far

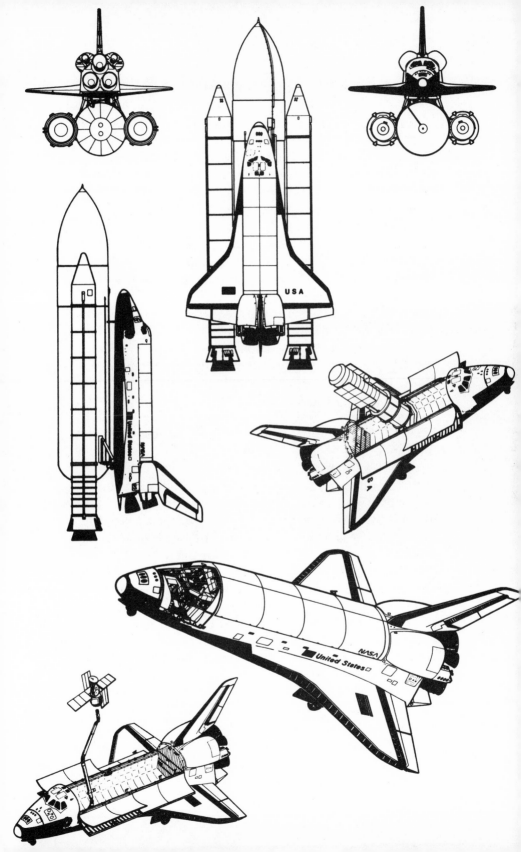

lower cost per flight than for previous launch vehi-cles.

Initially, NASA planned to build between seven and twelve orbiters (the fully reusable portion of the shuttle). Budget pressures, however, caused the fleet to be limited to six, then five, and eventually to just four. Cost-cutting also resulted in the elimination of jet engines to assist on landing, and restricted flights to a ten-day maximum. In addition, unmanned space tugs to carry payloads to higher orbits than the shuttle could reach had to be abandoned. Most of these design changes were made to reduce the development cost of the shuttle space transportation system, or STS. These cost-cutting measures were required because Con-gress placed a fixed ceiling on the shuttle's costs; therefore, as costs rose, capabilities had to be sacri-ficed. It is now generally recognized that the measures made to save on development costs have had the effect of greatly increasing the operations costs. Oper-ations costs refer to the cost per flight. As Dr. Logsdon has written, the shuttle "was designed to cost, not per-formance."[8]

The first space shuttle, *Columbia*, was completed in 1978 and was shipped in March of that year to the Kennedy Space Center for testing and its maiden voyage. Meanwhile, in 1977, the prototype shuttle *Enterprise* was used in a series of landing tests at Edwards Air Force Base in California. Although the shuttle program was planned to get off the ground in late 1979, technical difficulties with the main engines and the special "re-entry tiles," designed to protect the orbiter from the searing heat it would experience during its return to earth, caused repeated delays. In some respects, NASA underestimated the develop-ment difficulties of these high-technology systems.

As testing and final assembly continued, it became clear that the first shuttle flight would not take place in 1979 or 1980. Beginning in 1980, however, momentum toward a first flight increased as a series of complex tests were successfully completed. In early 1981, a test firing of *Columbia*'s engines was performed on the launch pad. Shortly thereafter, it was announced that the shuttle would make its first launch in April of that year.

SHUTTLE FLIGHTS AND
THE U.S. SPACE PROGRAM
IN THE 1980s

The first shuttle flight, STS-1, took place from April 12 to April 14, 1981. Since that time, flights of the space shuttle fleet have been the hallmark of U.S. space exploration. STS-1 ushered in the era of reusable space transportation and was widely hailed both in the United States and abroad. Coincidentally, the shuttle's first flight occurred on the twentieth anniversary of Yuri Gargarin's historic mission.

During 1981 and 1982, a total of four shuttle test flights were carried out. Each of these flights carried a crew of two test pilots, lasted for less than a week, and carried only simple payloads in the shuttle's cargo bay. All four of these flights used the shuttle *Columbia*. After the successful completion of the fourth test, NASA declared the shuttle "operational and ready for service."

In late 1982, the first operational flight of the shuttle, STS-5, was carried out; on this flight the shuttle launched its first communications satellite. In 1983, the orbiter *Challenger* was introduced into the fleet, and four more shuttle flights were made. In that year, crew size grew to as many as six astronauts. During 1982 and 1983 the shuttle routinely placed communications and scientific satellites into orbit. At the end of 1983, the European Spacelab research module was flown for the first time. In 1984, five flights were conducted, including two flights in which satellites were repaired in space. Also in that year, more satellites were deployed, and the third orbiter, *Discovery*, was declared ready for service. In 1985, a total of nine flights were conducted, with over forty astronauts flying in one year. During 1985, the fourth and final planned orbiter, *Atlantis*, was tested and then incorporated into the fleet. Also, three additional Spacelab research missions were carried out, and another satellite was repaired in orbit. Although critics claimed the shuttle was behind schedule and had nagging technical problems, the program as a whole seemed to be a success.

The U.S. space program flourished on other fronts as well in the early eighties. In the field of planetary exploration, a small NASA spacecraft called the *International Comet Explorer* made the first flyby and took direct measurements of a comet in 1985, and the much larger *Voyager* probes explored Jupiter (1979–1980), Saturn (1981–1982), and Uranus (1986). The earth was studied as well. Major NASA satellites were launched in 1981 and 1984 to explore the earth's ozone layer. One of these, the *Solar Mesosphere Explorer*, became the first NASA satellite to be operated by a university, the University of Colorado. To study the land and oceans, NASA launched two more *Landsats* and conducted a wide variety of remote-sensing experiments from the space shuttle.

In addition to manned spaceflight and scientific exploration, space utilization and commercialization became increasingly important in the 1980s. Private industry began to enter space in two ways. First, some firms began to market certain goods and services to the space industry; for example, McDonnell-Douglas sold booster rockets to take satellites from one orbit to another. Secondly, some other firms began selling or

Voyager 1 explored
Saturn in 1980.
This montage of
photographs shows
Saturn's rings and
moons. The Voyager
program has been
one of NASA's most
successful planetary
exploration missions.

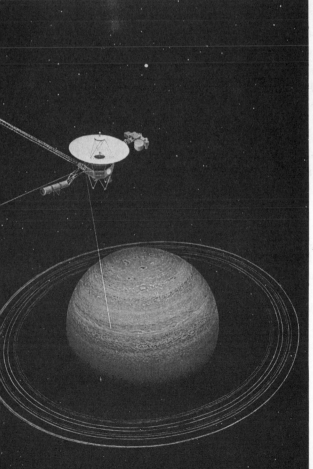

An artist's depiction
of Voyager 2
encountering Uranus
in January 1986

experimenting with sales of items made in space. Such "products" included photography for mineral exploration and communications satellites for business and residential use (including cable TV). Perhaps the boldest such effort came when the McDonnell-Douglas Corporation teamed up with Johnson and Johnson to produce certain drugs that could only be made in microgravity. For this project, a test plant was flown on six shuttle flights and a company engineer flew on three of these flights to monitor and optimize the production process!

FOREIGN EFFORTS
INCREASE AS WELL

Across the world, space programs expanded throughout the 1980s. The Soviet Union conducted more than a dozen long-duration space station flights and sent several probes to Venus and Halley's Comet. Plans were laid for a series of extremely complex missions to explore Mars and its moons. The Soviet Union also began developing the largest rocket in the world, larger even than the U.S. Saturn V had been. During the period 1980 to 1986, the Soviets averaged a launch rate of a hundred missions per year, more than five times the U.S. rate! In 1986, a new six-person space station called *Mir* (Russian for "Peace" or "World") was launched. According to Soviet space watcher James Oberg, *Mir* represents a new level of space applications and research that gives the Soviet Union capabilities in specialized research no other country has. By 1987, *Mir* was being manned on a full-time basis and expansion modules were being added. In addition to flight projects, the Soviets were also observed to be developing a space shuttle much like NASA's and laying the groundwork necessary for manned lunar and Mars missions.

In Asia, too, space activities expanded. China launched satellites regularly and developed sophisticated high-technology guidance and propulsion systems. The Japanese increased their efforts by building rockets of their own design, placing an emphasis on developing weather and earth-resources monitoring satellites and by participating in the U.S. manned projects. Even India began developing launch vehicles and satellites.

Europe became the strongest new space power of the 1980s. The European Space Agency conducted a wide variety of efforts. Foremost among these, of course, was the Spacelab research laboratory, which fit inside the shuttle. On one Spacelab flight in 1985, Europe actually rented (rather than shared) the entire shuttle and conducted dozens of its own high-technology experiments designed to improve Europe's industrial capabilities. Three European astronauts were sent on this mission. Additionally, Europe developed a large rocket called Ariane to compete with the shuttle and launched a number of scientific missions, including the *Giotto* probe to Halley's Comet. By the late-1980s, Europe was planning its own shuttle, building a much larger Ariane rocket, working to be a part of NASA's planned 1990s space station, and launching more than a dozen satellites per year.

AN ABRUPT HALT

As 1985 turned into 1986, the prospects for U.S. space exploration in the eighties and nineties looked the brightest they had been since Apollo. NASA was planning to launch the large and complex Hubble Space Telescope as well as carry out a mission to explore Jupiter in 1986. Plans were also being laid for a U.S./ international space station to be serviced by the shuttle. The long-awaited shuttle space tug, which was to serve as an extension of the shuttle to higher orbits, was under construction as well. Unmanned missions to map Venus and explore Mars were on the drawing board. The shuttle program was hoping to launch fifteen flights in 1986 and up to twenty-four flights per year by 1990.

Nineteen eighty-six began much as expected, with the launch of shuttle mission number 24 in early January. This flight was successful, and a second mission was planned for later in the month. Meanwhile, the Space Telescope was readied for a summer launch.

Less than three weeks after mission 24 landed, NASA proudly launched shuttle mission 25. The three-week "turnaround" time between STS-24 and STS-25 seemed to represent a new record in the interval between flights. However, as flight 25 climbed out over the Atlantic, it suddenly exploded and erupted in flames. With its crew and mission destroyed, the *Challenger* fell to the ocean. In the ensuing investigation into the destruction of the *Challenger*, many questions were raised about the conduct and purpose of the U.S. space program. In spite of its many successes, people still had doubts about it. For example: Why send people into space? Is what we learn in space worth the cost? Is the shuttle the proper kind of space transportation system? How could it be improved? What are our goals in space?

Before addressing these complex questions, however, we must first look at exactly what happened to *Challenger* and its crew.

C H A P T E R
T W O

CHALLENGER—
WHAT HAPPENED
AND WHY

AN OFFICIAL INVESTIGATION

Within hours of the explosion that destroyed the *Challenger*, public and congressional calls were heard for an official investigation. At NASA, Jesse Moore, the official in charge of the shuttle program, set up a "task force" to carry out a technical investigation of the cause, or causes, of the explosion. Moore's all-NASA team immediately impounded all data relating to the flight. Moore's team also initiated a salvage effort to recover as much of the wreckage as possible from the ocean, so that physical evidence would be available to help pinpoint the disaster's cause.

Still, there were calls for a non-NASA investigation. Such an investigation, it was said, would more likely be freer of bias than any investigation carried out by NASA or NASA contractors. Heeding these calls President Ronald Reagan, on February 3, 1986, appointed a group of thirteen distinguished engineers, test pilots, and scientists to investigate the *Challenger* accident. This group was officially known as the Presidential Commission on the Space Shuttle *Challenger* Accident. The commission's chairman was William P. Rogers, former secretary of state, former U.S. attorney

Some members of the Rogers Commission

general, and an accomplished lawyer. Other members of the commission included Neil Armstrong, the first man to walk on the moon; Sally Ride, an astrophysicist and the first American woman in space; and Richard Feynman, a physicist and Nobel Prize winner. Like the *Apollo 1* investigating committee, the *Challenger* commission was charged with carrying out a full assessment of all aspects of the accident and the shuttle program; unlike the *Apollo* investigation, the *Challenger* inquiry was performed publicly, by a basically non-NASA group.

The *Challenger* commission took testimony from over 160 individuals involved in the shuttle program and *Challenger's* last flight. More than 12,000 pages of sworn testimony was taken, and over 6,300 documents relating to the accident were reviewed. Over 6,000 engineers, scientists, technicians, and other individuals participated in the commission's work. On June 6, 1986, the *Challenger* commission released its final report, fixing the immediate cause of the accident as well as discussing the contributing factors that led to the wrongful decision to launch *Challenger* on January 28, 1986. The commission's report also made recommendations to improve the space shuttle's design and to prevent future accidents.

Using facts uncovered by the *Challenger* commission, as well as supporting evidence and eyewitness accounts of the accident and the salvaged wreckage, it is now possible to reconstruct the final flight of *Challenger* and the controversial events that led to it.

PREFLIGHT PLANNING

Challenger's final flight was officially known as STS-51L. Preparations for the mission began more than eighteen months before launch. When the flight crew was originally selected (January 27, 1985), 51L was scheduled to launch in the summer of 1985. However, schedule delays and a series of changes involving the cargo to be carried on the flight postponed the launch date to January 22, 1986. Because of these delays, both the detailed flight-planning process and the astronaut crew's training were delayed until an unusually short time before launch (about eight months). The commission noted that these delays, and the immense amounts of replanning associated with them, were a potential source of future problems.

The two major payloads carried on *Challenger*'s last flight were the second NASA Tracking and Data Relay Satellite (called *TDRS*) and the *Spartan-Halley* comet research observatory. In addition to these payloads, several small experiments were to be carried in the crew cabin.

According to preflight planning, mission 51L was to last six days. During this time the crew would launch the *TDRS* satellite, activate and launch *Spartan*, conduct astronomical and medical experiments, recover *Spartan* from orbit, and broadcast school lessons to students on the ground.

DELAYS AND DEBATES

From May 1985 until about a month before the actual launch, the launch date for 51L had held steady. Then, in December 1985, the preceding launch, STS-61C, slipped several weeks. This, in turn, caused 51L to be delayed from January 22 to January 26.

The planned 1986 shuttle launch schedule was very tight, and several high-priority missions were to take place in the early part of the year. Within NASA, plans were discussed to skip 51L if the launch date slipped beyond February 1 and proceed with the rest of the schedule. The purpose of such a move would have been to clear the pad for the next launch (an important mission scheduled for March) and to begin readying *Challenger* for its critical May launch of an international mission to explore Jupiter and the sun. If the May launch date were missed, NASA knew it would have to wait for more than a year for Jupiter to again be in proper alignment with the earth.

An afternoon launch was originally planned for 51L. Although scientists leading the Spartan project argued for retaining the afternoon launch, NASA mission planners insisted on changing the liftoff to mid-morning. NASA's reasoning for a morning launch was based on safety concerns. Were the vehicle to suffer an "engine-out" during ascent, it would have to glide

The crew of 51L, Challenger's last
mission. From left to right: Ellison Onizuka,
Mike Smith, Christa McAuliffe, Dick Scobee,
Gregg Jarvis, Ron McNair, and Judy Resnick.

to an emergency landing site at Casablanca on the west coast of Africa. Casablanca's runway was not equipped with night landing gear. Therefore, it was decided that the shuttle must be launched in the morning, Florida time, so that there would still be light in Casablanca, 4,000 miles (6,400 km) to the east.

The countdown for STS-51L began on January 26, but weather forecasts caused the launch to be postponed another day, to January 27. The crew spent the extra day reviewing flight plans and watching the Super Bowl from their quarters. During this period, pressures within NASA mounted. The *Spartan* satellite, which was to be put into orbit two days after launch required a launch either before January 31 or after February 6. With flights of even higher priority on tap, the prospect of canceling 51L became even greater. Every effort was made to make sure the shuttle would be ready on the twenty-seventh, when the weather cleared.

On the twenty-seventh, the vehicle was fueled, the crew inserted, and preparations made for a launch. Still, weather was a cause for concern. This time, rather than storms, there were high wind conditions. A decision was made to reschedule once again, for the next day.

During the evening of the twenty-seventh, and the early morning hours of the twenty-eighth, a series of meetings were held among NASA officials (mid-level managers from the Marshall Space Flight Center) and the shuttle's major contractors (Rockwell, Thiokol, and Martin Marietta). Marshall had final responsibility for the solid rocket boosters (SRBs). The purpose of these meetings was to assess the status of the launch. Such meetings take place during every mission countdown.

During these prelaunch meetings and a series of

phone calls, concerns about the possible effects of cold weather on the launch were expressed by some engineers from Morton Thiokol, the solid rocket booster manufacturer. In particular, Thiokol engineers Roger Boisjoly and Alan McDonald thought it possible that the booster's hot exhaust could "blow by" (get past) its protective seals, called O-rings, if the outside air temperature was too low. The reason why the O-rings might be bypassed was that they would become stiff in the cold. Once stiffened, the O-rings (which are supposed to be resilient) could not act to seal the SRBs. Without a good seal, exhaust would then leak out from the booster's side, rather than from the nozzle, and the booster would probably explode or rupture—ending the mission in catastrophe. In one conversation, Alan McDonald went so far as to say that if anything happened, he would not want to have to explain it to a board of inquiry. McDonald noted that no shuttle had ever been launched at a temperature below about 53°F, and that even at that temperature the craft had experienced some exhaust blowby.

The possibility of severe blow-by raised concerns and was the reason for many of the meetings that were held that night. Unfortunately, no actual tests of the boosters had ever been made at low temperatures and so there was no clear evidence of what would happen. For this reason, Thiokol engineers recommended the launch be delayed until later in the day, or perhaps until January 29.

However, NASA managers, feeling increasing pressure to launch, pressed for a firm "Go or No Go" from Thiokol. In testimony to the Rogers Commission, NASA managers later stated that the probability of an O-ring failure was believed to be low and that each O-ring was "backed up" by another for increased protection, in case blow-by did occur.

Perhaps sensing the impatience of some NASA officials, particularly Lawrence Mulloy, Thiokol managers overruled their own engineers and signed a form stating the SRBs were "Go" for launch. Without such a signature, the launch could not have been held.

THE FINAL COUNTDOWN

During the final hours leading to the launch of STS-51L, all of *Challenger's* mechanical and electrical systems were checked. The crew was awakened about six that morning. Because there was a buildup of ice on the launch pad and some delays in fueling the huge external tank, the launch was delayed first from 9:38 to 10:38, then to 11:38. To some extent, these piecemeal delays were unprecedented in the STS program. Several of the onboard scientific experiments required launch times earlier than 10 A.M. (on any given day) in order to function in orbit. These experiments were "sacrificed" in order to get the flight launched that morning. Clearly, NASA wanted to get 51L flying, so that it would not be canceled altogether.

By 8:36 A.M. the astronaut crew had arrived at the pad and boarded the shuttle. The countdown proceeded normally.

As the final few minutes passed, Pilot Mike Smith powered up *Challenger's* turbines for flight. Only two minutes before launch, Commander Scobee called to astronaut Ron McNair, engineer Greg Jarvis, and schoolteacher Christa McAuliffe on the shuttle's lower passenger deck: "Two minutes, downstairs. Anybody keeping a watch running?"

At launch minus thirty seconds, *Challenger's* onboard computers took control. First, the orbiter's three powerful main engines were pressurized, then thousands of electronic checks were performed to verify they were ready to start. On schedule at minus 6.6

seconds, the main engines were ignited, one at a time, about a second apart. *Challenger's* computers quickly evaluated the running temperatures and pressures of each engine, and when 90 percent of flight level thrust was reached on all three, the command was sent to ignite the SRBs. Both SRBs ignited simultaneously, and the vehicle rose from the pad. On board, astronaut Judy Resnik exclaimed, "Aaall Riiight!" as *Challenger* began the long-awaited push to orbit. In the launch control center 3 miles (4.8 km) away, Boisjoly and McDonald let their breath out—apparently the O-rings would hold. The temperature at the base of the pad was 38°F.

THE SHORTEST FLIGHT

As *Challenger* rose, things looked fine from the cockpit, from the launch control center, and from Houston; they looked fine to McDonald and Boisjoly, too, and to the crowds of onlookers who attended the launch. Things looked fine, but they were not fine.

Less than a half-second after the SRBs ignited, the first of eight small but ominous puffs of black smoke swirled from one of the lower joints in *Challenger's* right solid rocket booster. These puffs were not obvious to onlookers but were recorded by cameras filming the launch. Later analysis by technical experts working with the presidential commission revealed that a primary O-ring had failed to seal in the right SRB and that its backup O-ring had failed as well. Blow-by had occurred! Engineering analyses later indicated that either propellant residue or O-ring soot plugged this leak about 2.5 seconds into the flight. Like blood from a wound, the blow-by had formed a scab that stopped the flow.

Experienced shuttle launch watchers claim 51L was the loudest shuttle launch they had ever heard.

Spartan-Halley's project scientist said at the time, "It sounded ominous—almost evil." Today it is believed that the launch was louder to spectators because the cold air carried the sound better.

For nearly a minute, 51L's ascent went as planned. *Challenger* rolled to put itself on the proper flight path, checks of onboard systems showed no "anomalies," and the vehicle properly throttled back its engines as planned when aerodynamic forces built up.

About fifty-nine seconds into launch, however, trouble began. A review of film from ground cameras recording the launch again detected flames coming from the right SRB. *Challenger* was being buffeted by a combination of high-altitude winds and the period of greatest aerodynamic stress during launch. In response the vehicle flexed a tiny amount and began to steer its engines to counteract the wind. In combination, these forces probably reopened the wound in the right SRB caused by the blow-by at ignition. Over the next five seconds the plume of flame grew and grew. By sixty-four seconds, a gaping hole was forming in the casing of the SRB. The thrust escaping through this hole exerted a force of 100,000 pounds on the shuttle, greater than the thrust of many jetliners. *Challenger's* computers interpreted this force as unusually strong winds. To counteract the 100,000-pound (45,000-kg) side force, the shuttle swung its engines slightly to the left. Inside the cockpit, the crew was jolted around by a combination of actual wind gusts, engine steering, and the thrust escaping from the breeched SRB. Pilot Mike Smith remarked, "Got a lot of winds up here today."

At seventy-two seconds into the flight, the 3,000°F exhaust from the right SRB either tore or burned loose the attachment strut between the SRB and the external tank. In the final second of flight, computers on board *Challenger* detected a fuel line break caused by the widening explosion and shut down each of the shuttle's three main engines. A moment later, the SRB slammed into and tore off *Challenger*'s right wing, then careened into the tank, setting off a massive explosion that destroyed the orbiter. Simultaneously, the cockpit voice recorder taped the first and last indication that anyone on board had of serious trouble— Pilot Smith, either seeing the SRB veering toward him out his window or noting the red engine shutdown lights on his control panel said "Uh oh." At an altitude of 48,000 feet (14,600 m) and a speed of Mach 2 (twice the speed of sound), *Challenger* broke up.

On the ground, some spectators realized that the SRBs had separated too early. Others, not that familiar with shuttle launches, didn't even know anything was wrong—at least not right away. Soon, however, it was clear to all that the shuttle was nowhere to be seen in a widening fireball and that the SRBs were wildly spinning off on their own, still under thrust.

At Mission Control in Houston, telemetry signals suddenly stopped. At first, having seen no indications of trouble during the launch, flight controllers believed that either the tracking station or the shuttle's radios had failed. Within seconds, however, radar tracking detected hundreds of pieces of debris following *Challenger*'s trajectory. Noting this, Flight Dynamics Officer Brian Perry, a veteran shuttle flight controller, confirmed the data and announced in chilling words over an internal NASA communications channel, "The vehicle has exploded."[1]

THE COMMISSION FIXES BLAME

The *Challenger* commission made a methodical study of all the events leading up to the flight of STS-51L. They also evaluated flight records radioed to the ground, debris recovered from the ocean, and film of the flight taken by long-range cameras. Many individuals were interviewed, and a great number of technical studies were performed to test theories concerning the in-flight events of January 28.

The commission considered many possible things that could have caused Challenger's destruction. Included as possibilities were a failure of the main engines; a rupture of the huge external fuel tank; a problem in one of the payload rockets (such as the ignition of the TDRS satellite's upper stage); a failure in one of the SRBs; premature ignition of the shuttle's emergency destruct system; and sabotage. As the evidence mounted, many of the possible causes were eliminated from the list. By early February, just weeks after the launch, the investigators were already focusing their entire attention on the right SRB. Much of the reason for this early narrowing of the possibilities came about because films (from automatic cameras) developed after the flight clearly showed black smoke seeping from SRB joints at ignition and these films also depicted bright flames jetting from the rocket casings beginning around launch plus fifty-eight seconds. Engineers and technicians working for the commission considered propellant cracks, rocket motor case cracks, and O-ring seal problems as possible causes of the SRB failure. In its final report, the commission pinpointed the cause of the accident and made several recommendations for improvements in the shuttle and its management.

The telltale puff of black smoke can be seen coming from the right solid rocket booster in this photograph, taken moments after launch.

From a technical standpoint, the cause of the disaster was quite clear. The commission stated, "the cause of the accident was a failure of the (O-ring) pressure seal . . . of the Right Solid Rocket Motor."[2] In reaching this conclusion, many possible SRB "failure modes" had been evaluated. Once the O-ring was identified as the cause, the commission went on to determine what specifically caused the O-ring to fail.

Again, many possibilities were checked. Had the O-ring been improperly installed or tested? Had sand or water gotten into the O-ring joint to prevent it from sealing? Had the cold been to blame? Had the elastic putty used in the O-ring joint failed to seal? Again, more tests were performed, and the flight data and debris were reanalyzed. However, the commission was not able to make a definite conclusion about this. Too much of the evidence had been destroyed in the explosion. Although it was certain that the right SRB had experienced a failure in one of its joints, it was possible that one or more of the above causes were to blame. The commission did, however, conclude that the SRB design was prone to certain kinds of failures, including the one that destroyed *Challenger*.

MANAGEMENT PRESSURES CONTRIBUTE TO THE ACCIDENT

The *Challenger* commission's findings went far beyond a determination of the immediate cause of the accident and technical recommendations to solve the cited problems. The commission also concluded that there had been "serious flaws in the decision-making process" leading to 51L's launch. In particular, they concluded that exceptions to established rules had been granted "at the expense of flight safety" and that

Morton Thiokol's management "reversed its position and recommended launch . . . contrary to the views of its engineers in order to accommodate a major customer [NASA].[3]

Regarding this last point, it was found that previous ground tests and blow-by problems experienced on past flights should have alerted NASA and Thiokol to the serious deficiencies in the SRBs. The commission also found that the Marshall Space Flight Center had not properly passed evidence of SRB problems up the chain of command within the shuttle program but had instead, "attempted to resolve them internally."[4] The commission stated in its report to the president that this kind of management "is altogether at odds with . . . successful flight missions."[5]

GETTING THE SHUTTLE
BACK ON TRACK

After analyzing the cause of the *Challenger* disaster, the presidential commission made a number of recommendations to NASA. These recommendations fell into several categories, including the SRB's design and shuttle management. The goal of the recommendations was to improve the reliability of the entire shuttle.

In particular, the commission recommended that the SRBs be redesigned and recertified to solve the numerous problems inherent in their O-ring joints. The redesign specifically called for an SRB that in future flights would "be insensitive to"[6] environmental factors, including the cold and rain as well as "assembly procedures."[7] Further, the commission called for a design that would have joints as strong as the rocket casings themselves. To verify the integrity of the new design, the commission recommended testing full-size boosters before the new SRBs be committed to actual flight. These tests began in the summer of 1987.

In addition to recommendations concerning the SRBs, the commission also made several specific recommendations relating to other potential problem areas in the shuttle. They insisted that the shuttle's brakes be improved (a long history of brake problems had occurred over many flights) and that a reevaluation of crew abort and escape mechanisms be undertaken to determine if launch and landing problems could be made "more survivable." Finally, the commission insisted that the rate of shuttle flights be controlled to maximize safety. Such a policy had not been implemented in the past, the commission said.

Going beyond technical matters, the presidential commission recommended a number of sweeping changes in the shuttle program's management structure, designed to prevent the problems that led to a "flawed decision-making process"[8] regarding the launch of 51L. These specific recommendations included the establishment of a safety panel with broad powers reporting directly to the manager of the shuttle program and the establishment of an Office of Safety, Reliability, and Quality Assurance within NASA reporting directly to the NASA administrator, with broad powers to investigate and demand solutions to safety-related issues.

Additionally, it was recommended that a full review take place of all critical safety items in the space shuttle before the next flight. Finally, the commission recommended that astronauts be more fully involved in the shuttle program's management. This recommendation was in response to the anger expressed by some astronauts during the investigation that they, who were at greatest risk in each flight, had not been informed of the O-ring blow-by and erosion problems prior to the accident. In response to this call,

NASA placed senior astronauts such as Bob Crippen, Sally Ride, Charles Bolden, and Paul Weitz in key oversight roles.

TWO OTHER IMPORTANT
ROCKETS FAIL

Clearly, the loss of the space shuttle *Challenger* in January 1986 was a serious blow to the U.S. space program. However, while it did severely limit the ability of the United States to operate in space, it did not shut it down completely. A few unmanned rockets (which had once been the backbone of the NASA and military space programs) still remained available to launch certain critical satellites. However, by presidential order, these rockets were being phased out in favor of the shuttle. Only a few medium-capability Delta and Atlas launch vehicles and a handful of powerful Titan launch vehicles remained at the time of the shuttle accident. The first launch after the shuttle disaster was scheduled to take place in April.

This launch used a Titan rocket to carry a secret military satellite. Titans had flown over a hundred times, almost always with success. The April launch was particularly important to military planners because it reportedly carried the replacement for an aging spy satellite.

Careful preparations for the Titan launch were made. By the morning of April 16 all was ready, and the huge Titan was launched. But less than 1,000 feet (300 m) in the air and only seconds into its flight, the Titan exploded, destroying its payload and heavily damaging its launch pad. Immediately, the Titan program was grounded and an investigation was called for. Counting a previous launch in mid-1985, two Titans had blown up in a row. No two Titans had blown up in a single year since the 1960s!

This failure shocked the aerospace community and placed the country in great danger. The secretary of the air force told the Senate that the shuttle and Titan failures together constituted a "national emergency." With both the STS and Titan grounded, the United States had no way of launching heavy military satellites to replace aging ones in orbit.

Less than a month later, on May 3, NASA conducted its first launch of a satellite since *Challenger*. Riding atop a Delta rocket on this flight was a new weather satellite. In 177 launches, only five failures of the Delta had occurred, the last in 1978. Still, NASA conducted special tests and simulations to ensure the Delta's readiness for this important flight. Yet only seventy-one seconds after the launch, the Delta suddenly shut off. The vehicle's self-destruct was then activated to prevent it from falling on populated areas. Again, a previously reliable rocket had failed and an important satellite was lost. Delta flights were grounded; another investigation team was called in.

THE OVERALL IMPACT OF SHUTTLE AND ROCKET FAILURES ON THE SPACE PROGRAM

The twin failures of the older launch vehicles, following closely on the heels of the *Challenger* disaster, ground the U.S. space program to a halt. With no way of launching new satellites into orbit until these rockets were recertified for flight, both NASA and the military were "pinned down." New research could not be conducted. Replacement military and weather satellites could not be launched. New space missions backed up in a long line awaiting launch. By late 1986, the situation reached near-crisis proportions. Many scientific payloads were canceled, or delayed for years! Military planners were forced to buy dozens of expendable Titan and Delta rockets. And U.S. commercial communications satellites were left without a choice but to fly on the European Ariane rocket.

As the shuttle, Titan, and Delta investigations dragged on, it was asked whether there was a common thread that might tie the multiple failures of proven systems together. Officials investigated this possibility but could find nothing. Both NASA and the air force officially claimed there was no relation between the failures. Unofficially, however, some veteran aerospace engineers suggested that the streak of "bad luck" might indeed be more than that and that the "unprecedented" run of mishaps might have been precipitated by the decision to curtail unmanned rockets in favor of the shuttle. Their scenario goes as follows.

As pressures increased to make the shuttle the primary U.S. launch vehicle, safety concerns in the 51L prelaunch meetings were discounted in order to meet scheduling demands. Mission 51L exploded as a result. Simultaneously, with fewer and fewer unmanned launches scheduled, the quality-control practices of rocket manufacturers may have become lax. Perhaps worse still, many experienced launch and checkout engineers left industry during the phaseout of unmanned rockets. Together, these factors may have conspired to cause the back-to-back rocket failures. All in all, sources say it looked like a case of too little foresight on the part of key space planners in the White House and Congress. In late 1986, a congressional investigation came to this same conclusion, finding that outside pressures on NASA to fly the shuttle more and more often set the stage for the accident.

ARE WE DOING ENOUGH?

Given the severity of the Challenger and other rocket accidents, we must ask ourselves whether the measures being taken to correct the problems are sufficient.

In the case of the space shuttle, most attention is being focused on fixing the immediate cause of the accident—the solid rocket boosters. However, additional efforts are being made to improve the shuttle's brakes, to review all critical systems for design flaws, and to take a fresh look at crew escape provisions. Effort is also going into improving management and communications within NASA.

What else could be done? What else should be done?

The most important fact overlooked in this period of "blame fixing" is that the shuttle has flown twenty-four times and is a proven system. In fact, statistically, it has proven itself to work as well (96 percent of the time) as do our most reliable unmanned rockets. Because of the shuttle's extreme complexity, however, it is also important to realize that any change, including improvements, will introduce new possibilities for failure. Therefore, improvements and changes must be made very carefully and only when absolutely necessary.

Still, with proper concern for introducing additional "failure modes," some measures could be taken to enhance the shuttle's overall reliability and flight safety. One important area of concern is the shuttle's main engines. These high-technology workhorses have required much more maintenance after each flight than predicted. Efforts should be made to improve engine life and reliability; such modifications would also make the process of preparing each shuttle flight simpler, since the need for complex engine overhauls and testing could be reduced.

Concerning escape measures, many studies have been performed in the aerospace industry and in NASA. All of these have shown that adding escape systems to the shuttle would be difficult, costly, and very time-consuming. Some studies have found that adding an escape system could add up to two years additional delay to the program. Still, certain simple measures are under consideration and could be implemented to give crew members a better chance of survival in an accident. One step already approved is to equip the orbiter with an explosive (quick-opening) hatch and an escape slide to promote easy escape in a landing accident or during an ocean ditching. Currently, crew members must manually open a complex hatch and then shimmy down a rope. Clearly, in a situation requiring quick escape, this would not serve the needs of injured crew members and may not even be adequate for the others. Also, it has been suggested that crew members return to wearing pressure suits during launch and landing. Although heavy and bulky, they would provide protection against any loss of cabin pressure, such as that experienced by *Challenger*'s last crew.

Finally, in the area of shuttle hardware improvements, more spare parts are sorely needed. Often, one shuttle must be "scavenged" to obtain parts for another shuttle about to fly. According to workers, this scavenging creates delays (because of the time that must be taken to remove the part from the working orbiter). As an example, on its last flight *Challenger* flew with orbit control engines borrowed from *Discovery*. In addition to causing delays and extra work, the borrowing of parts from one vehicle to fly another also increases the risk in each flight. The dismantling and reassembly of a working shuttle to fix a problem in another increases the probability that both vehicles will later experience problems. The shuttle program needs more spare parts, particularly for engines, turbines, and key electronic components.

Although modifications to the shuttle itself can

add to the risk of failure and should only be implemented as required, many deficiencies have been pointed out in the facilities that support the shuttle, such as its launch and landing site facilities. For example, consideration should be given to improving the runway and navigational facilities at emergency landing sites, to bring them up to par with the main landing sites at Kennedy Space Center and Edwards Air Force Base. Had Casablanca had runway lighting, an afternoon launch, with warmer conditions, would have been possible.

Another improvement needed in the shuttle system concerns the launch pads. At the Kennedy launch center, large shuttle-enclosing buildings should be constructed to protect the STS from wind, rain, and cold before launch. Such a pad enclosure has been developed for the Shuttle Launch Complex at Vandenberg Air Force Base. Had such a device been available for 51L, rain could not have seeped into the SRB joints, and the cold prelaunch temperatures would not have affected the SRBs.

It is clear that each of the above measures would add cost to the shuttle program. Unfortunately, many of the shuttle program's previous bad decisions have come from a lack of funding. In several instances, the *Challenger* commission found that improvements and design changes that were needed were not implemented because of a lack of money.

If NASA is to have a safe and efficient shuttle, it must make its full budget needs known to Congress and the president. This has not always been clearly communicated in the past, the commission found, and is a potential source of safety problems.

Finally, going beyond hardware modifications and improvements, several changes to the shuttle's "operations philosophy" are needed. Chief among these is the recognition that the shuttle is an experimental vehicle and as such should not have to meet a clock-work schedule. In any developmental program as complex as the shuttle, the world's first reusable spaceliner, delays and technical difficulties are to be expected. In 1982, the shuttle was declared "operational" after only four flights. This premature move was made to appease shuttle critics who wanted the program to start "turning a buck" or be canceled. In the future NASA must not trade flight safety and a careful development program for short-term economic gain—or an on-time schedule. The loss of a space shuttle orbiter and its crew, and the delays in space activity, are too great a risk. Implementing such a philosophy means providing better crew training, more simulators, and an upgraded Mission Control. Flight controllers for 51L used the same equipment as did their counterparts in Apollo, some seventeen years before! This is one reason why indications of trouble did not appear on flight monitor screens until a careful playback after the explosion.

Changing the operations philosophy also means planning a (reduced) series of flights and then sticking to them. The presidential commission found that most shuttle flights were replanned at least once, often with additional experiments or payloads (and sometimes even crewmembers) added shortly before launch. The commission found that this kind of flexibility is not appropriate for a developmental program like the shuttle and greatly contributes to the complexity of flight operations.

Taken together, this series of recommendations implies a different kind of shuttle program, not the routine transportation to orbit that was once the shuttle's primary goal. If the shuttle is to be truly successful, it must operate with safety and efficiency, and on a reliable schedule; these goals translate into additional dollars and cents for the program.

As revealed in testimony to Congress and the Rogers Commission, the shuttle program was severely underfunded during its development and early flights. This underfunding caused many decisions to be made on economic rather than safety factors. The decision to keep the shuttle flying with O-ring problems in 1985 was made, at least in part, on this basis.

After the shuttle accident, the American Institute of Aeronautics and Astronautics (AIAA) criticized the U.S. space program as "severely underfunded."[9] The AIAA consists of over 40,000 aerospace engineers and scientists. According to their report to Congress, NASA's budget is about half what it was in the Apollo era, while its responsibilities have increased. As a nation, the United States is faced with deciding whether or not the space program warrants increased funding.

C H A P T E R
T H R E E

WHY EXPLORE
SPACE?

Spaceflight is a very expensive enterprise. Since its inception, NASA has spent over $200 billion (inflation included) on space. The Department of Defense has spent at least as much on space as NASA, and several other government agencies such as the National Oceanographic and Atmospheric Administration have spent billions of their own.

Are we getting our money's worth? What benefits have come to society as a result of our space programs?

THREE BROAD MOTIVATIONS
FOR EXPLORING SPACE

The reasons to explore and exploit space fall into several categories. First, there are the philosophical reasons—the desire to explore and to seek out new perspectives on our world and our lives. James Michener, the famous American novelist, summarizes this viewpoint by saying, "In every generation one field of exploration ends . . . (and) we start something new."[1] This perspective is called the "manifest destiny" approach to space advocacy. In the 1800s, manifest destiny was defined as a God-given imperative for exploring and settling the North American continent. It was in this vein that newspaper editor Horace Greeley motivated western settlers in the 1840s when he said, "Go West, young man!" As it relates to space, this viewpoint advocates space exploration because some people want to do it and because these people feel a need to explore, to push back frontiers, and to expand human activity into new realms.

Edward Lindaman, a former aerospace industry executive and author, advocates another widely held philosophical view. Lindaman says space should be explored because unexpected good will come of it. Lindaman's perspective is held by many advocates of the space program and may be called "blind faith" advocacy. Lindaman uses the story of Michael Faraday, one of the pioneers of electricity, to illustrate his view. When invited to appear in front of the British Parliament 120 years ago and explain the usefulness of electricity, Faraday could not say what the uses would be but predicted, "Someday you will tax it."[2] The blind faith advocates point out that many inventions, ranging from electricity to the laser and the airplane, were first believed to have no "practical benefit" and that the most important benefits of space exploration will come about in time.

A variation on blind faith was expressed by William Bainbridge in his book, *The Space Flight Revolution: A Sociological Study.* Bainbridge argues that spaceflight is actually a twenty-first century enterprise born "before its time" for political reasons (that is, American and Soviet competition) but important to continue because the reasons for doing so will become clear in hindsight.

Although both manifest destiny and blind faith each hold some merit, they rely upon the conviction that space exploration is inherently good for the long-

The Hubble Space Telescope, pictured in this artist's conception, will give astronauts the best-ever view of the universe. NASA plans to launch the observatory on the fifth shuttle mission after flights resume.

term future of humankind. A more concrete motivation for the exploration of space cites the need for scientific discovery and invention to advance society. This line of reasoning predicts that space exploration will improve our future. Although this view relies upon an element of blind faith, it has been well supported by the first thirty years of space exploration. Using satellites and manned spacecraft, the world's weather patterns, its mineral and agricultural resources, and even its ocean currents have been mapped. Scientific discoveries in space have led to an understanding of the problems humans have caused by polluting the earth's air and water. The exploration of the planets has taught us much about the workings of the earth—its atmosphere, geology, and history. Some even claim that the ecology movement got increased attention when the first pictures were taken of the earth from space, showing it as a fragile planet orbiting in the darkness. Similarly, the engineering challenges of building spacecraft and managing large space projects have demonstrably spurred the computer industry, electronics miniaturization, solar energy production, the development of strong and light-weight materials to replace steel, and medical technology, to name some prominent examples.

An even more specific line of space advocacy points to the long list of direct benefits that space exploration has already produced: worldwide telephone communications, sports and news programming from other nations, weather forecasting, crop monitoring, earth-resources programs, and navigation satellites that have improved air transport, shipping, and trucking. There are satellites to monitor arms treaties and to guard against surprise attack; satellites that track the geological tensions that lead to earthquakes; satellites that locate airplane- and shipwrecks within minutes, and the list goes on.

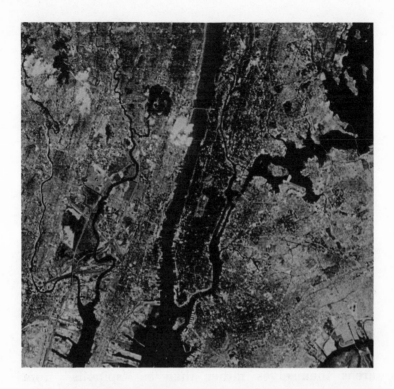

Landsat *photographs have pioneered observations of the earth from space. This* Landsat *photo is of Manhattan in New York.*

SPACE CRITICS HAVE GOOD ARGUMENTS

Given such an overwhelming set of benefits and such lofty goals as manifest destiny, one might ask why there is any debate at all about the usefulness of our space program. Still, there are critics of space exploration. In response to the broad philosophical motivations and tangible benefits offered by space advocates, space critics point out the harsh realities of today's world.

The primary criticisms of the space program are twofold: that government expenditures in space are at the expense of more important programs and that space exploration can wait. More specifically, critics claim that humankind today faces many pressing problems, and the exploration of space diverts money, resources, and human talent away from these problems. Space program critics point out that the total space expenditures of the United States today exceed $20 billion per year and that that amount could go a long way toward eradicating hunger or pollution. Some space critics of the 1970s, such as Senators Edward Kennedy, Walter Mondale, and William Proxmire, have advocated the total elimination of spending on space except for weather and defense satellites.

Space program critics also dispute the contention that space produces unexpected "spinoff" benefits. They argue that the same results might have been achieved more effectively by research in the needed areas themselves rather than as "spinoffs" from space.

Other critics question whether space activities such as the Apollo moon program or the shuttle are necessary. These critics claim that most technologies and discoveries have come from the more modest projects, such as communications satellites.

Such criticisms are valid. In a world of limited budget resources, space exploration does indeed take away from other programs. Programs such as weather and communications satellites, although less exciting, have provided more direct benefits than have the larger, more glamorous projects.

Some space advocates, such as author Ben Bova, president of the National Space Society, counter critics by insisting that space is a long-term investment. Historically, however, the United States has not

NASA has launched scientific satellites to study the earth, the planets, the stars, and the sun. The small satellite shown here was launched in 1981 to monitor changes in the earth's protective ozone layer.

invested in long-term enterprises. Most business and economic planning takes place on a yearly, or even shorter, basis. Bova's call to "invest in space" for the future hearken back to blind faith and manifest destiny.

If space is to gain a strong foothold in our society, then we must reap its benefits in the present rather than in the future. As we will see in Chapters Five and Seven, some elements of the space program are already trying to make this change come about.

WHAT ARE THE
REAL DEBATES?

Why are we in space? The answer appears to be that we are in space because the U.S. government believes it is in our best interest to be there. In 1986, the *Congressional Record* included testimony supporting our reasons for being in space, including national prestige, for the increased expansion of the national economy, to motivate students in their studies, to invest in the future, to improve industry's technological base, and "to provide services for the good which could not be accomplished otherwise." Space policy analyst Dr. John Logsdon advocates space exploration on the basis that it is "high culture."[3] Though not specifically mentioned, one must also include in this list the oldest (and perhaps still the most valid) reason for exploring space: competition—not political, but economic. Many countries believe space is important to their economic future (see Chapters Five and Seven). Studies in the United States have shown this to be true.

Given that space does indeed return many benefits and that space exploration is important to future economic and technological advance, experts such as Neil Hosenball, former director of the University of Colorado's Center for Space Policy, say that the debate is not *if* but *how* we should explore space.

The "how" is indeed the hard part. Answering this question requires deciding both how we shall pay for space exploration and what kind of exploration we should pursue. For the near term, we shall continue to pay through taxes. In the future space industrialization may, as did the settling of America, pay its own way.

C H A P T E R
F O U R

WHAT GOOD
ARE PEOPLE
IN SPACE?

Since the earliest days of the space program, debates
have raged about the importance of using people to
explore space. In some circles, manned spaceflight is
seen as the crowning achievement of space exploration, while other groups see the manned effort as a
show that diverts needed resources from more useful
applications and explorations. In this chapter we will
explore this debate.

ADVOCATES OF UNMANNED
PROGRAMS CITE COST
SAVINGS AND SAFETY
AS ADVANTAGES

As early as the Eisenhower Administration, the need
for manned spaceflight was questioned. However,
when it became clear that the Soviet Union planned to
put people in space, American public opinion de-
manded that the United States do it also. With this in
mind, the Eisenhower Administration started the
Mercury program. Following Yuri Gagarin's historic
flight, President Kennedy asked for and got a larger
commitment to manned exploration, including the
Apollo moon-landing effort. Throughout the 1960s,

the manned Gemini and Apollo programs dominated the U.S. space effort.

After the moon landing was achieved, however, those favoring an unmanned program once again made their case. Scientists such as Thomas (Tommy) Gold of Cornell University and Dr. James Van Allen, the discoverer of the earth's radiation belts, spoke convincingly on the greater usefulness of unmanned probes. In the scientific community, the belief was (and still is) widely held that manned efforts are too expensive and that they drain needed dollars from other programs, such as planetary exploration. A more cost-efficient space program with greater direct benefits to the public could be achieved, some believe, without any manned exploration at all. Critics of manned flights also point out that unmanned space activities are far safer than manned explorations, since (by definition) no lives are at risk.

Dr. Bruce Murray, a former director of NASA's Jet Propulsion Laboratory, recently pointed out that unmanned communications satellites are the only projects to have returned a profit from space, and that weather, navigation, and search and rescue operations are all made possible by satellites. Dr. Murray summarizes his findings as follows: "Except when the purpose of space flight is the political and psychological one of human adventure and exploration . . . the optimal human role is to remain on the ground." To further support his view, Dr. Murray notes that the U.S. military has never needed or used manned spacecraft to conduct its missions.

Critics of the "unmanned only" view say that limiting ourselves to unmanned explorations would be, quoting author Ben Bova, like sending "Lewis and Clark out to explore the Louisiana Territory, but then forbidding settlers from going West."[1] Although the advocates of unmanned spaceflight are correct in stating that most discoveries and most tangible benefits have been brought about by unmanned efforts, it is also often true that the advocates of the unmanned approach are usually either seeking to reduce the overall size of space exploration efforts in the United States or are themselves directly involved in unmanned missions.

WHO FAVORS
A MANNED FUTURE
IN SPACE?

The advocates of manned spaceflight are a varied group. Included among them are those who wish to go into space themselves, those who believe that manned spaceflight is essential to national prestige, and those who simply feel that without manned spaceflight the whole effort has no ultimate purpose.

In a recent poll of its membership, the Planetary Society, a space advocacy organization primarily interested in solar system exploration by unmanned probes, found that the great majority of its members wanted to see manned flight continue after the *Challenger* tragedy. Other space organizations have found similar desires among their members. Time and again, letters and comments accompanying such polls mention manned flight and human expansion into space as the key benefit derived from space exploration.

This kind of response indicates that the public sees space exploration differently than do many scientists and legislators. National public opinion polls have demonstrated that few private citizens are aware of the unmanned program and its many benefits. This is most likely because people identify with people in space, rather than with machines. Although the tangible benefits of manned spaceflight cannot measure up to those of unmanned efforts, there are intangible benefits, such as national pride, technological development, and the thrill associated with manned spaceflight that unmanned efforts cannot capture. Along these lines, Dr. Harlan Smith, director of the McDonald Observatory and a planetary astronomer, has summed up the position of many by saying, "Without manned exploration, the unmanned program would wither away, lacking the support provided by the more visible manned efforts."[2] Dr. Smith cites support for his view in the fact that budgets for unmanned programs have risen and fallen with the fate of manned exploration budgets and that unmanned efforts have never gained increased support when manned exploration has been cut back.

PEOPLE AND MACHINES
EACH MAKE UNIQUE
CONTRIBUTIONS

Clearly, both manned and unmanned spacecraft have their own unique attributes. Unmanned missions can go to places people cannot, such as faraway Jupiter or the fiery surfaces of Venus and Mercury. Unmanned missions can last much longer than manned flights and are therefore better suited for routine astronomical and earth observations. Also, because people's movements and even their sneezes can upset precise sensors, unmanned spacecraft can point their instruments more accurately. Unmanned missions also generally cost less than manned missions, primarily because they do not require elaborate safety systems and use smaller ground support teams. In sum, unmanned spacecraft seem ideally suited to making astronomical observations, exploring the planets before humans are sent, monitoring the environment and the weather, and providing communication and navigation services.

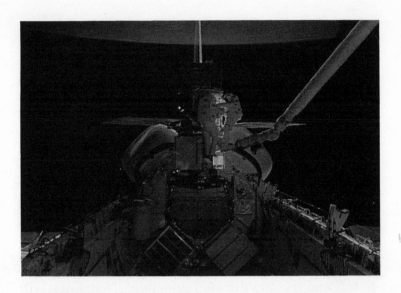

On several flights, NASA has used the shuttle
to repair ailing satellites. In this picture, taken
in 1984, two astronauts are shown working on
the disabled Solar Max observatory.

Manned missions exhibit one unique attribute—
they carry people, and people are better suited than
machines to make judgments and draw conclusions
from observations. Manned flights are therefore far
superior to machines in modifying the course of an
experiment based upon findings. People are also useful for making unplanned observations and for repairing instruments when they fail. In-flight repairs saved
the Skylab space station from certain failure after
launch, and in 1984, astronauts repaired a disabled
$100 million satellite called Solar Max. A recent
NASA study called "The Human Role in Space" concluded that people excel in jobs involving judgment
and dexterity and in instances when unforeseen
occurrences require quick actions. Therefore, it seems

that people are best suited for roles such as developing new products in space (see Chapter Seven), in conducting complex scientific experiments such as from the proposed space station or Spacelab, in repairing satellites, and in building large facilities in space.

Finally, only manned missions seem able to inspire the public and motivate students and educators. Unfortunately, it is also true that only manned flights can result in the kinds of tragedies typified by the *Challenger* accident.

Summing up, it therefore seems that in the near term, people are best suited to "operations" in space, while machines are best suited to providing routine or extended services. In the longer term, people will join machines in the exploration of the planets, and if computers and robotics develop sufficiently, machines will join humans in the industrial development of space. Dr. Paul Scully-Power, a former Australian citizen and oceanographer who rode aboard the shuttle, sums up the roles of people and machines as follows: "Exploring space by means of both manned and unmanned systems provides a synergistic effect that transcends the results obtainable by either alone."

ALTERNATIVE OUTCOMES

As the space program recovers from the *Challenger* accident, the debate between manned and unmanned exploration will probably continue. One of three broad outcomes are likely to emerge in the end: a heavy reliance on manned exploration, a heavy reliance on unmanned exploration, or a balanced approach. Each of these alternatives will produce its own outcome. What might result from each approach over the next ten years?

In a primarily manned environment, the space program would most likely consist of the space shuttle

Plans for the first permanent U.S. space station were started in 1984. By 1994 the facility should go into operation. By contrast, the Soviet Union has launched some eight space stations already, two of which are operating today.

and the space station. Unmanned weather and communications satellites would continue as well, but new programs such as extensive earth science explorations, new *Landsat* craft, and the development of unmanned observatories and complex missions to the planets would suffer. However, manned high-altitude missions to communications satellite orbits 22,300 miles (35,680 km) up might be made to repair and refuel existing satellites. Scientific missions would probably continue using a variety of shuttle and space station experiments. Given such a program, the development of advanced interplanetary propulsion systems and new rockets would not occur. The great benefits from this approach would come from manufacturing discoveries made aboard the space station, as well as lessons learned about our ability to operate for long periods in space.

In a primarily unmanned program, the shuttle would probably continue, but the space station would not be built. Unmanned explorations of the planets would increase, leading to probes that would sample the atmosphere of Saturn, return soil samples from Mars, and perform detailed studies of comets and asteroids. Larger and more complex space observatories would also be launched. In this scenario, a greater reliance would be placed on expendable rockets as well, and several new ones might be designed to meet the needs of the expanded fleet of unmanned spacecraft. Manned missions would be used to repair, refurbish, and refuel unmanned craft in low orbit, but not much higher, since this would require the development of new manned spacecraft. Manned scientific missions would probably be used only to conduct experiments requiring human judgment or intervention, such as for the development of new alloys or pharmaceuticals in microgravity.

In a balanced approach, new manned capabilities such as the space station and perhaps a new space tug to reach high orbit would probably be developed. Unmanned explorations of the planets would continue at a slow pace, and soil samples from Mars and complex new missions to the outer planets would probably be sacrificed.

Each of these approaches has its own merits. However, unless the space program's budget grows dramatically, any of these scenarios will involve hard choices. Which course the nation takes is up to its leaders, its citizens, and the needs of the economy for space development and international competition.

CHAPTER FIVE

PROBLEMS IN SPACE TRANSPORTATION

Space transportation systems must include the launch vehicles used to lift spacecraft into orbit and the upper stages used to move satellites between orbits. They also should include transportation to the 22,300-mile- (35,680-km-) high "geosynchronous" orbit used for communications satellites and the powerful high-energy stages used to push interplanetary probes out of earth orbit on trajectories toward Venus, Mars, Jupiter, and beyond.

The key requirement of a space transportation system is the safe delivery of payloads to orbit. Because of the tremendous energies and complicated technology involved, most forms of space transportation have proven to be only about 90 to 95 percent reliable. When space transportation is not reliable, the rocket and payload end up either destroyed in a launch accident or adrift in a useless orbit.

SPACE TRANSPORTATION
1960 TO 1985

In the 1960s and 1970s, launch services were provided by the governments of the United States and the Soviet Union, and each country developed a stable of launch vehicles. These "national" rockets ranged from small satellite launchers up to the mighty Saturn-class vehicles NASA produced to put *Apollo* on the moon. The largest Saturn rocket, the Saturn V, was capable of putting 300,000 pounds (133,000 kg) into earth orbit and just over 100,000 pounds (45,000 kg) on a course to the moon. The Soviets attempted to build a Saturn V-like rocket called the "G Booster" in the late sixties, but they were unsuccessful.

At the end of the Apollo program, the United States decided to develop the space shuttle. As discussed earlier, the space shuttle was to drastically cut the cost of space transportation by being reusable, unlike any previous rocket. The shuttle was also designed to repair satellites in orbit and to return nonfunctioning satellites to earth for refitting. Both of these capabilities were incorporated to further reduce the cost of space transportation. According to estimates made at the time, the shuttle would be able to carry all government and commercial payloads planned and foreseen for the eighties and nineties. Although the shuttle was designed to carry only 65,000 pounds (29,000 kg) into orbit (as opposed to the 300,000 pounds, or 133,000 kg, of the Saturn V), the Saturn program was canceled. This decision saved money but left the United States without a heavy-lift launch capability.

As the shuttle was developed, several measures were taken to reduce its cost. First, jet engines were removed; then the fleet was cut in half. Finally, its long-term mission and high-altitude capabilities were removed. In a further cost-cutting move designed to shore up political support for the shuttle, President Jimmy Carter officially directed all other U.S. launch vehicles to be phased out and all U.S. payloads to fly on the shuttle.

Meanwhile in Europe, the ESA made "independent space access" one of its main goals for the 1970s. To do this, ESA developed the Ariane to carry European and other international satellites into space. Ariane was to be a special-purpose vehicle, designed primarily to launch communications satellites to geosynchronous orbit. The Ariane family of launch vehicles ranged from the *Ariane 1* and *Ariane 2*, which could put a few thousand pounds into such an orbit, to the *Ariane 4*, which could put up over 9,000 pounds (4,000 kg). Ariane was not designed to carry people. Therefore, its development was simpler and less expensive than the shuttle.

It could be said that the United States was attempting to design an "all things for all people" spacecraft, a versatile, heavyweight launch vehicle that could carry people, experiments, and satellites into orbit. By doing this and by getting rid of all its other launch vehicles, the United States put all its eggs in one basket. The Europeans, by contrast, designed a special-purpose launcher specifically to meet the needs of European industry. Because Ariane was not reusable, the loss of any one vehicle would not affect the fleet's future capabilities. Both the shuttle and Ariane, it was hoped, would eventually make a profit from their launch services.

Being simpler and less costly to develop, Ariane was the first to fly. The first two Arianes were launched in 1979; two more were launched in 1980. Although one of these four vehicles exploded on its way to orbit, an aggressive sales campaign produced a large number of orders for the Ariane.

The shuttle program got underway with two launches in 1981 and three more in 1982. In 1982, Ariane suffered a second launch failure, and because of the resulting launch backlog, Europe was forced into buying one of the last surplus U.S. Deltas to launch an ESA satellite.

As the shuttle and Ariane each gained more experience, launch rates increased. Each program garnered about half of the commercial satellite launch business, and the race seemed about even. The U.S. military, however, came to believe that the shuttle would never reach its goal of twenty-four flights per year. The reasons for this were complex but centered on the fact that the shuttle was much more difficult to operate and service than had been anticipated. Also, NASA had been allowed to build only four shuttles, not the seven to twelve originally planned. With fewer shuttles to fly and each flying less often, the U.S. launch capacity was limited. Because it was realized that any shuttle accident might seriously impair U.S. space activities, the air force was authorized in 1985 to build ten new rockets, called complimentary expendable launch vehicles (CELVs). The word "expendable" is used to denote a one-time-use vehicle. The Titan launcher was selected to become the CELV. These rockets are to begin flying in 1988, in order to give the United States a backup to the shuttle.

In addition to the government-sponsored shuttle, the CELV, and the Ariane, the early 1980s also saw the first attempts by U.S. private industry to offer launch services. Several small companies designed new rockets to put small satellites into orbit. The best known of these companies is Space Services International (SSI) of Houston. Financed by Texas oil millionaires, SSI launched its first test rocket in 1982. Private companies also took over the defunct Titan, Delta, and Atlas launch vehicles that the government had abandoned for the shuttle.

To encourage these private efforts, the Reagan Administration sponsored key legislation and instituted the Commercial Expendable Launch Vehicles

Activities Executive Order of 1984. This legislative package was partly an attempt to streamline commercial launch vehicle sales and operations. The Department of Transportation was to oversee the effort and all future commercial launch activities. Also, in 1984, NASA established an Office of Commercial Programs to stimulate commercial interest in space.

Even with this help, however, none of the commercial launch vehicle companies sold any rockets. Quoting Ariane's chief representative in the United States, Ian Pyrke, "until the *Challenger* accident, it looked as if American efforts to commercialize expendable [launch vehicles] . . . were going nowhere." One reason for this was that both the Ariane and the shuttle were heavily subsidized by their governments. That is, both the shuttle and Ariane were able to charge less than full price for launches, with tax dollars making up the difference. Because the new launch vehicle companies could not charge prices as low as the shuttle or Ariane, they failed to get customers.

MULTIPLE FAILURES ROCK SPACE TRANSPORTATION

As we saw earlier, in 1985 and 1986 an unprecedented string of launch vehicle failures rocked the aerospace community and the world. Within the space of nine months, two Titans, one Delta, two Arianes, and the *Challenger* all blew up. Shortly thereafter, in early 1987, an Atlas launch vehicle lost control less than a minute after its launch and had to be destroyed. The shuttle program was halted. The Titan, Atlas, and Delta programs were also stopped while investigations took place. Ariane's failures put it on hold for the rest of 1986 and most of 1987. In the entire Western world, access to space was halted. Even the U.S. Atlas program was subject to failure, and only a few Atlases were left. Secretary of the Air Force Edward Aldridge said he believed the decision to phase out launch vehicles other than the shuttle had not only left the United States without backup but had indirectly contributed to the Titan and Delta failures. Aldridge claimed that the phaseout of unmanned vehicles had caused many of the best rocket engineers, some of them twenty-year veterans, to leave these programs.

In the aftermath of these failures, it became apparent that the decisions that had led the United States to rely solely upon the shuttle had been shortsighted. In the United States, military, commercial, and scientific satellites were left stranded on the ground, without transportation to orbit. In fact, the combined storage and maintenance costs for the many grounded satellites exceeded $50 million a month!

1986: A YEAR OF CHANGE

In the aftermath of the shuttle disaster, the goals of the shuttle program were drastically revised. With only three orbiters and a two-year delay in flights, a large backlog of payloads accumulated. Although NASA was authorized by President Reagan to replace *Challenger*, funding and technical problems will delay the completion of the new shuttle until at least 1991.

To make up the backlog in payloads awaiting launch, several major decisions were made. First, the shuttle has been prohibited from entering into any new contracts for the launch of commercial communications satellites. Also, the shuttle's most powerful upper stage, the Centaur, will be abandoned for safety reasons. Centaur's development cost NASA over a billion dollars, even though it was never used. Its cancellation caused the scientific community considerable pain, since many planetary exploration payloads require the Centaur in order to be flown. Now, these payloads will have to be redesigned and/or wait a long time for the first of the new rockets to come off the assembly lines.

Also in 1986, all plans to launch the shuttle into polar orbit from a California launch base were indefinitely postponed. This move will limit the shuttle's usefulness but will make possible more flights. This is because basing all the orbiters at Kennedy is more efficient than spreading them (and their support crews) between two launch bases.

To make up for lost shuttle launch capacity, the air force and NASA each purchased additional unmanned rockets. The air force bought over two dozen Martin Marietta Titans and a dozen Deltas; NASA bought two McDonnell-Douglas Deltas. This helped remove some of the backlog of military satellites that had planned to fly on the STS. The air force and NASA also encouraged commercial industry to take up the slack by agreeing not to compete in the arena of commercial satellite launches.

These moves could help get the U.S. commercial launch industry on its feet. Less than six months after the shuttle accident, Martin Marietta Corporation sold the first commercial launch vehicles in the United States. By contrast, in the three years prior to the tragedy, they had sold none. In the post-51L environment of increased reliance on expendable vehicles, companies offering newly designed rockets also have a better chance to make sales. Late in 1986, Hughes Aircraft Company, one of the largest satellite builders in the world, and the Boeing Corporation offered to build an entirely new *large* launch vehicle of their own. Hughes named this project "Jarvis" in honor of Gregg Jarvis, the Hughes engineer who died aboard *Challenger*. The Jarvis launch vehicle is planned to lift heavy commercial and military satellites into orbit

Among the U.S. launch vehicles that have been commercialized are the already developed Delta, Atlas, and Titan, and several smaller new projects such as the Industrial Launch Vehicle and the Conestoga. Most commercial rocket launches will orbit communications satellites.

and should equal the Titan and exceed the shuttle in terms of payload capacity. Later in 1986, in what was perhaps the most daring commercial space launch business move of all, four different corporations offered to buy their own shuttles and operate them for profit! Unfortunately, legal issues relating to the sale and use of shuttles ended these attempts to commercialize the shuttle.

By convincing the government that it was too risky to rely upon just one launch vehicle for all space transportation, the shuttle disaster may ultimately have put the United States on a much stronger footing. Unfortunately, however, things will not get better very fast. The first of the new U.S. expendable launch vehicles will not be ready until at least late 1988, more than two years after the shuttle accident.

One of the greatest problems that came out of the string of failures from 1985 to 1987 was the devastation of the launch insurance business both in the United States and abroad. Prior to 1985, satellite owners could insure their payloads for as little as 5 or 6 percent of their replacement cost. In this way a satellite owner could be protected against a launch failure. In 1984 and 1985, however, $632 million in claims were made for lost satellites, while only $194 million in premiums had been paid. Because of these great losses, insurance rates skyrocketed 20 and even 30 percent. Some insurers dropped out of the launch insurance business altogether. At such a high cost for insurance, satellite operators found it less expensive to build extra satellites in case one failed to reach orbit than to pay for insurance. These problems in the insurance industry severely hampered the ability of the Titan, Delta, and Atlas launch companies to get customers. In Europe, however, Ariane offered its own insurance (through government backing). This gives the European launch system a double advantage—insurance and subsidy. Still, the Ariane's poor record (four failures in eighteen flights) remains a drawback to its customers.

As mentioned in Chapter One, several other countries had also jumped into the fray. Seeing the prestige and profits associated with space transportation, Japan, China, and India each developed the advanced technologies once held only by the United States and the Soviet Union. Japan, for instance, is building a new booster called the H-2 to compete with Atlas, Ariane, and Delta. The Chinese government aggressively sought out U.S. communications satellites for launch on their Long March series of boosters. A Swedish firm and a Houston communications satellite company each signed up for Chinese launches. Space policy expert Neil Hosenball has called the Chinese move "a real threat"[1] to the commercial success of the U.S. launch industry. Even the Soviet Union began offering its large Proton booster for hire.

FUTURE TRANSPORTATION NEEDS MAY NOT BE MET

Looking to the future, the United States may have even greater problems competing in space transportation than it has today. The Soviet Union is now developing a new Saturn V-class booster, as well as both a minishuttle and a large shuttle much like our own. In Europe and in Japan, plans are on the drawing board for shuttles. As NASA wrestles with its recovery from the *Challenger* explosion, other countries are quickly moving to get new, more sophisticated, and more powerful launch vehicles built.

According to military sources and the prestigious *Aviation Week* magazine, by 1990 the Soviet Union will probably be capable of launching a dozen shuttle flights and two or three large Saturn-like flights per year. This is in addition to the hundred-plus launches they now conduct each year with ELVs. The European shuttles now being planned include design features far in advance of our shuttle, which was designed in the early 1970s. Japanese plans include a minishuttle capable of transporting people to and from space stations.

Given the current budget deficit problems of the U.S. government, it is unlikely that the United States will soon construct either a new heavy-lift launcher (like the Saturn V) or a new generation of more efficient shuttles, even though both are severely needed and have been strongly endorsed by industry. To illustrate this situation, President Reagan's request for funding to *just study* an advanced shuttle called the National Aero-Space Plane (NASP) was severely cut back in the 1987 and 1988 federal budgets.

Peter Gwynne, a senior editor at *High Technology* magazine, recently wrote, "If the U.S. doesn't begin to confront [these issues] . . . others will grasp the opportunities. . . . Then the launch vehicles, factories, and space settlements of the 21st Century could be dominated by foreign companies, just as the driveways of well-to-do U.S. suburbs are today filled with BMWs, Volvos, and Mazdas."[2]

C H A P T E R
S I X

SPACE COMMERCIALIZATION: PROSPECTS AND PROBLEMS

A SPACE INDUSTRY WAITING IN THE WINGS?

Arthur C. Clarke, writer and theoretical inventor of the communications satellite, said, "Space flight, if it is to continue, needs a more stable basis."[1] Many believe that a more stable basis will come from the transition from government to private sector activities. This is the process of space commercialization.

In the past ten years or so, NASA has placed stronger emphasis than ever before on the economic returns space could bring to the nation's economy. For example, space offers certain unique advantages such as microgravity, an almost perfect vacuum, and a vantage point high in the sky. Each of these advantages can be translated into commercial products and profits. Additionally, with the advent of the shuttle, industries wishing to manufacture goods or provide services in space felt that they could, for the first time, count on routine transportation to their orbiting investments.

The history of space commercialization stretches back over twenty-five years. During most of that peri-

*Australia's AUSSAT communications
satellite leaves the cargo bay of the
earth-orbiting* Discovery *on mission 51I.*

od, however, the only viable commercialization of space took place in the field of satellite communications. By 1980, satellite communications had become a $3 billion per year industry. The early success of communications satellites in the 1960s spurred the development of several support industries. For example, communications satellite manufacturing companies were formed by Hughes Aircraft, RCA, and the Ford Aerospace Corporation. To date these firms have built over a hundred commercial communications satellites. The launch insurance industry (discussed in Chapter Five) developed to provide financial coverage against the risks involved in communications satellite launches. In addition to insurance companies and satellite builders, commercial ventures were formed to produce rocket stages such as McDonnell Douglas's PAM (payload assist module) to take communications satellites to high orbit.

Although the satellite communications industry prospered, no other commercial applications of space emerged until the early 1980s. The change came about with the advent of the space shuttle. Given the potential returns from space and the success of the early shuttle flights, many businesspeople saw space as the coming wave. Peter Glazer, vice president of the prominent consulting firm Arthur D. Little, summed up this sentiment by saying, "Space in the 21st century will probably be what aviation, electronics, and computers were . . . in this century."[2] Art Dula, a prominent attorney specializing in space law, was quoted in 1984 as saying, "The next generation of billionaires is going to come from the business of space."[3] Milt Copulos, of the Heritage Foundation, said the same year, "No matter what we think the figure is today [for space profits] . . . we are grossly underestimating the potential."[4] Given this kind of optimism and the success of the early shuttle flights, many new space ventures began to emerge. Companies began to make plans for microgravity manufacturing projects, acquiring earth resources and weather satellites, providing launch services for hire, and even selling burials in space!

SPACE COMMERCIALIZATION
EFFORTS IN THE UNITED STATES

No less than six broad categories of space commercialization exist in the United States today. To date, over $15 billion in revenues have been generated by space-related business ventures. The Center for Space Policy (CSP) in Cambridge, Massachusetts, predicted that by the year 2000, existing and new space ventures could produce between $16 and $51 billion in revenues.

What kinds of ventures are now operating or will someday be operating in space? As previously mentioned, the space communications industry is the strongest. According to David Lippy, president of the Center for Space Policy, communications satellites are now a "mature industry," exhibiting strong growth and considerable profits. In addition to providing the long distance telephone and television services most people associate with communications satellites, space communications also provide special business data transmission services as well as location and navigation services that are revolutionizing the shipping and trucking industries. In addition to communications, space transportation and "materials processing" are each trying to emerge as profitable fields. The space transportation industry, which was discussed in the previous chapter, is today in a state of flux because of the many changes associated with the *Challenger* disaster and other rocket failures. Although this new industry had no success selling rockets prior to the shuttle accident, it is now expected to grow considerably as the United States diversifies its space transportation systems beyond the shuttle. NASA estimates that up to 200 rockets and upper stages will be needed to launch communications and other satellites between 1987 and 1990.

In another area, experts agree that materials processing in space holds more long-term growth potential than any other endeavor, except perhaps tourism (which will have to wait until the next century). Materials processing involves developing new products, such as revolutionary drugs or alloys, in the microgravity of space. In order to develop space products for sale on earth, much research is needed.

Unfortunately, the infrequent opportunities to do industrial research on the shuttle (an average of five or six experiments per year, so far) have severely hampered the start-up of materials processing in space. To date, only two materials processing efforts have been commercially successful. In the first, Particle Technology, Inc., of Pennsylvania, produced millions of nearly perfectly formed "microspheres" for research labs on earth; such perfect microspheres cannot be made on earth. The second success is McDonnell Douglas's Electrophoresis Operations in Space (EOS) processing lab. EOS has flown on six shuttle flights. Using a procedure known as "space electrophoresis," McDonnell Douglas and a group of business partners have been able to produce chemicals and drugs that are extremely difficult to make on earth. In one experiment, the EOS factory produced the blood clot remover erythropoetin 700 times as fast as on earth, and at five times the purity! Until the *Challenger* accident McDonnell Douglas was planning to begin human testing of the drug in 1987.

Given their success with erythropoetin, McDonnell Douglas hopes to be producing up to fifteen separate products with space electrophoresis by the mid-nineties. Other companies, such as Deere and Company, 3M, and General Motors, are now entering the materials processing field. However, these firms have only conducted preliminary research and have not yet developed any products from their activities.

In addition to materials processing, space transportation, and space communications, remote sensing from space has also begun. Remote sensing is the business of using satellites to survey the earth. Such spacecraft have been employed to conduct oil and mineral searches, guide ships through the icy Arctic, monitor crops, and track huge schools of fish.

The commercial remote-sensing industry only got under way in 1985, when the federal government turned over the *Landsat* earth-resources satellites to private industry. EOSAT Corporation now operates the existing *Landsats* and is planning to build and operate up to two more. Because it is unlikely that there will be any profits from these ventures, the government is subsidizing EOSAT for its first few years. Congress approved the subsidy because, in the long run, it was less expensive to subsidize the start-up of EOSAT than it was to continue running the *Landsat* program itself. EOSAT is now selling high-resolution images of the earth to farmers, to land-use planners, to governments, and even to the news networks! Although EOSAT has not yet operated the *Landsat* system at a profit, several small private firms are now using data from *Landsat*. And, as in the space transportation field, Europe is also pursuing the commercialization of earth resources.

The final area of space commercialization being developed today is the space services industry. This industry consists of firms providing space hardware or services for use in space. Examples include Astrotech International, which provides private satellite ground servicing; Spacehab Inc., which is building a private-use laboratory for experimentation aboard the shuttle; Space Industries, Inc., which is building a space factory that will be leased to materials processing concerns beginning in 1992, and MRA Inc., a small Florida firm that plans to rent materials processing furnaces to companies wanting to try new techniques aboard the shuttle. In another "services" venture, the Celestis Group of morticians is offering burial in space for those who wish to have their remains cremated and put into permanent orbit. Because many firms operating in this field sell their products to other space ventures, such as materials processing communications satellite companies, space services as an industry has made a good start.

SPACE COMMERCIALIZATION IN EUROPE, JAPAN, AND RUSSIA

Outside the United States many space commercialization efforts are under way as well. European industry is planning to begin materials processing activities soon. To get experience in this field, the ESA bought a shuttle flight, STS-61A, and loaded it full of experiments in alloy and electronics manufacturing. This flight took place in late 1985 and was extremely successful. Plans for a follow-up flight in 1989 and another in 1992 are now proceeding. Additionally, the ESA wants to manufacture materials both on the U.S. space station as well as on its own *Eureka* satellites in the 1990s. Japan is planning to send astronauts on a shuttle flight in 1990 to begin experimenting in this field and is also planning to place a major facility for experimentation and production aboard the U.S. space station. The Soviet Union has a large materials processing effort, which is conducted by cosmonauts aboard their *Salyut* and *Mir* space stations. It is estimated that the Soviets have conducted over 1,500 materials processing experiments; by comparison, the United States has conducted about a hundred. The Soviets have reported sales within the Soviet Union of alloys, electronics crystals, and even medicines made in space.

With regard to remote sensing, European industry is also now operating its own earth-resources satellite system for profit. This system is known as the Satellite Positioning and Tracking (SPOT) project. SPOT satellites have superior resolution to the U.S. *Landsats* (that is, they can detect smaller objects on the ground).

In its first year of operation, 1985, SPOT sold millions of dollars worth of images to European, U.S., and Asian customers, including the U.S. Department of Defense! In Japan, a series of earth-resources satellites was inaugurated with a 1987 launch. These satellites will focus on water resources, including ocean fisheries, which are important to the Japanese economy. In the Soviet Union, remote sensing is developing, but it is hampered by government security restrictions.

As described in Chapter Five, commercial transportation systems are being built and sold by many countries, including European nations, the Soviet Union, and China. Europe is also getting into the space services market by leasing space on its newly planned *Eureka* space satellites. *Eureka* will directly compete with the planned American facilities for materials processing.

THE DIFFICULTIES WITH
SPACE COMMERCIALIZATION

Although space commercialization is gaining a toehold in the U.S. economy, several problems could prevent it from ever becoming big business. In the near term, space business prospects suffer from the reduced confidence of American industry in NASA. This has arisen as a result of the *Challenger* accident and the management problems discovered by the *Challenger* commission. In the longer term, the great problems facing commercialization involve the perceived and actual risks of doing business in space. Most investors shy away from space business ventures because they view it as too risky and also much more expensive than most business ventures on earth. It costs millions of dollars to develop a space payload and millions more to orbit it. Wolfgang Demisch of First Boston Corporation of New York sums up the situation: "In space, you can't start small and grow."[5] Worse still, getting into space involves about a one in twelve chance the payload will be destroyed in a launch failure.

Yet another risk inherent in any space business is the likelihood that launch failures can temporarily and unpredictably halt access to space. The Titan, Delta, Ariane, and shuttle failures of 1986 combined to deny access to space by businesses for more than a year. This situation makes it almost impossible to conduct business in a competitive world. Coupled with the high costs of space business, these risks discourage all but the most promising space ventures.

In addition to the risks involved in space activities, three other serious problems face space commercialization. First, the regulatory and legal environment is not conducive to business. For twenty-five years, space was the province of governments alone, and a "climate" for business has not been established yet. One example of this involves products produced in space aboard the shuttle which, until recently, were charged import duties because they were "produced out of the country"; this added to their cost and made space products less competitive with those made on the ground. Another problem is that business ventures in space (such as remote sensing and space transportation) often find themselves competing against subsidized foreign enterprises. Such subsidies have been offered by foreign governments to improve the competitive positions of their own companies. The U.S. government has not offered subsidies except in the form of certain breaks on launch costs and a direct payment to EOSAT, Inc., for taking over the remote-sensing program.

The final problem facing potential space businesses is the cost of getting into space. With launch costs near $2,000 per pound, only a very few products can be made in space at a profit. Space experts have calculated that any product manufactured in space needs to be worth at least $3,000 per pound to be profitable. This is several times the price of gold! Therefore, until space transportation costs drop, very few space products will be made at all. Taken together, these obstacles indicate that space commercialization has a long way to go before it can succeed.

NEW ACTIONS COULD FOSTER SPACE COMMERCIALIZATION

What could be done to improve the outlook for space commercialization? Clearly, the most important efforts center around space transportation. Routine access to space must be assured, and the cost of getting payloads to orbit must be drastically reduced. The risks of a space launch must also be greatly reduced. With these changes, more potential ventures would meet the test of profitability, and more businesses would be willing to invest in space ventures.

How could space transportation be made reliable, dependable, and less expensive? To begin, the United States must have a robust and diverse series of launch vehicles so that a complete standstill like the one that occurred in 1986 cannot occur again. One recent action taken by the government to foster space commercialization was the decision to allow NASA and the military to lease launch pads and other facilities to commercial companies. This will improve the launch vehicle industry's prospects, since it means they do not have to re-create the facilities owned by government before beginning launches.

The United States must also make a long-term commitment to developing the next generation of space transportation systems, with much lower operation costs. Vehicles now on the drawing boards should be able to get factories and other space businesses into orbit at about $200 per pound rather than $2,000 per pound, as it now is. The newly started National Aero-Space Plane program is aimed in this direction, as are the European Sanger and HOTOL concepts. If the United States fails to build second-generation shuttles such as these, space may be the province of our foreign competitors.

Another action the government could take would be to ensure the timely construction of the U.S. space station. The space station will greatly enhance prospects for commercialization by improving the transportation system and by giving space manufacturing a long-term base of operations. It will improve space transportation for two reasons. First, payloads will have a place to go to, rather than depending upon short shuttle flights. Secondly, payloads to be used aboard the station will need only one launch in order to operate. By contrast, shuttle payloads must fly again and again to accumulate time in space. Because of its permanent nature, the space station will also be able to operate its payloads for long periods. After all, operating for a week-long shuttle mission once or twice per year is no way to run a factory. Jerome Smirnoff, vice-president of CitiCorp Industrial Credit, summed up the feelings of many space investors when he said, "Other than communications satellites, you won't see a flood of space-oriented deals until the space station is in orbit."[6]

In addition to improving space transportation and providing a space station-like industrial park for development, the U.S. government will also need to reduce the bureaucracy where space is concerned and eliminate outdated statutes. In particular, experts insist that the tax code needs reform. Fortunately, this effort is already under way.

IS SPACE COMMERCIALIZATION
IN THE PUBLIC GOOD?

Is space commercialization in the public interest? It seems so.

A survey of Fortune 500 companies showed strong support for it, President Reagan is firmly behind it, and the U.S. Congress has passed supporting resolutions.

What specific benefits does space commercialization hold for the public? Protection against foreign competition will be one important benefit, as will the introduction of new products and services to the economy. The ultimate success of space commercialization will be that government operations in space, both by NASA and the military, will become cheaper, because competition will force down the prices for satellites, launches, and other services. The successful commercialization of space will also mean that our investment in space activities will have created new jobs.

Historians tell us that over 80 percent of all jobs available today are in fields that did not exist a hundred years ago. The new drugs, alloys, metals, electronics, and communications services (such as "Dick Tracy" style wristwatches that will allow phone communications with anyone in the world), will each fuel the economies and industries of the twenty-first century. Even space tourism could become a reality if space transportation costs and risks are substantially reduced.

Have efforts at space commercialization occurred too soon? Probably not. The current problems are pointing out that space is really still a new field. We will have to learn how to do business there, just as we once did with interstate commerce and the distribution of public utilities.

CHAPTER SEVEN

WHY DO SPACE PROJECTS COST SO MUCH?

A space shuttle orbiter costs over $2 billion. The Hubble Space Telescope costs over $1 billion, and a typical scientific satellite costs about $300 million. Commercial communications satellites cost $20 to $70 million. By contrast, the entire Mercury space program cost only about $100 million in current dollars, and typical scientific satellites in the 1960s cost millions, rather than hundreds of millions, of dollars. With the costs of space projects increasing and NASA's relatively low budget, policymakers have recognized the fact that NASA may soon not be able to afford any new projects at all!

WHY ARE SPACECRAFT SO EXPENSIVE?

Why are space projects so expensive? One reason is that space missions have become more complicated than they were in the early days of the Space Age. Compare the shuttle orbiter and a Mercury capsule, for example. Mercury capsules had the ability to ride into orbit atop a rocket, sustain human life for about a day, conduct simple experiments inside the cabin, and return to a watery landing somewhere near a waiting ship. By contrast, the shuttle can take a crew of nine into orbit under its own power, support them for over a week, rendezvous with other spacecraft, conduct complex experiments, carry up to 30 tons of equipment into space, and return to a runway landing. Clearly the 150,000-pound (67,000-kg) shuttle is much more complex that the 4,000-pound (1,800-kg) Mercury capsule. Similarly, the Hubble Space Telescope and other modern scientific satellites are also many times more complex and sophisticated than their less expensive predecessors.

Added complexity aside, what factors contribute to the high costs of space exploration? Studies have examined the breakdown of costs in a typical satellite project. Those factors that were found to be important were the "do it all yourself" nature of spacecraft design, the "custom assembly" of satellites, and the great amount of travel expense incurred when NASA and its contractors are separated around the country.

One underlying reason spacecraft are expensive is that they are, in effect, self-contained traveling worlds. Unlike a new building on earth, spacecraft can't plug into the power grid and the telephone network, or count on the solid earth to orient them properly. Instead, all of these services and others (such as air, food, water, and waste disposal on manned missions) must be provided by the spacecraft itself. Each satellite must bring along everything it will need for its entire operating life (plus backups in case something fails). Providing for all these services is estimated to account for one-half the cost of each satellite mission. This is the "do it all yourself" dilemma of spacecraft design.

A second reason why spacecraft are so expensive is the "custom assembly" problem. Custom assembly comes about because almost every spacecraft built for

NASA today is a one-of-a-kind item. In the 1960s and early 1970s, many space projects involved the launch of a series of two to ten similar satellites, each with different experiments but with a similar spacecraft "bus." Examples from that era include the Orbiting Astronomical Observatory program (which involved three satellites) and the Orbiting Solar Observatory project (which included nine nearly identical spacecraft). Today, the Hubble Space Telescope program, like the Mars orbiter, the space station, the Gamma Ray Observatory, and most other projects, consist of just one spacecraft.

One-of-a-kind "custom built" spacecraft projects incur high costs for two reasons. First, all of the design and testing needed to bring the new satellite into being must be spent on a single craft. This is rather like paying for all of an automobile's design and testing costs yourself, rather than sharing those costs with other customers! Another factor introduced by custom-designed single-satellite systems is that, with only one chance to get it right, NASA is forced to conduct many more tests and do a more in-depth analysis of the design than it might if there were many satellites in each project. This increased amount of testing is needed to make sure the spacecraft will work properly on the first try, because no backups exist.

Why build only one vehicle in each program? Because it is too expensive to build more than one spacecraft each on NASA's small post-Apollo budgets! This vicious circle feeds itself; costs rise, so one-of-a-kind spacecraft are built, causing the cost per spacecraft to rise further.

The final reason why spacecraft are so expensive is the high cost and great amount of travel that takes place between NASA and its contractors. A typical two-engineer trip that lasts four days costs the taxpayer about $1,500. More than a thousand such trips have been logged for some satellite projects, tens of thousands in the construction of a shuttle. A solution to this problem would be to "co-locate" NASA management at the various industry design and manufacturing facilities needed for a given project, so that travel costs would be minimized.

INNOVATIVE IDEAS
HAVE BEEN TRIED

In the 1970s NASA recognized the escalating costs of space projects. Since then, several efforts have been made to correct the basic problems outlined above.

In an early attempt to lower costs, NASA began a trial program to see how inexpensively a small (1,000 pound, or 450 kg) scientific spacecraft could be built. This project, called the Solar Mesosphere Explorer (SME), was started in 1978. SME was designed to study the earth's ozone layer. To save on travel expenses, the entire spacecraft was built by various companies and a university group, all of which were located in one place—Boulder, Colorado. Proven designs were used so that development and test costs could be kept to a minimum. To save even more, the satellite was operated by college students at the University of Colorado at Boulder, rather than by highly paid aerospace engineers. This was and is the only time NASA has let college students operate a NASA satellite. Altogether SME cost about $17 million, less than half of the cost of similar satellites. From this experiment, NASA proved that innovative design, contracting, and operations could dramatically cut spacecraft costs.

Another idea NASA has tried to cut costs is the MMS, or multi-mission spacecraft. All MMS satellites carry standard data-handling circuitry, tape recorders, and pointing control systems. It was reasoned that using standard MMS parts for some of the most widely

In the Solar Mesosphere (SME) project, NASA allowed the University of Colorado to employ college students to operate the satellite. This project successfully demonstrated one way of cutting satellite costs.

used systems would help get away from the "custom satellite" dilemma. With many different spacecraft using common components, NASA hoped to cut hardware costs by spreading hardware design and test costs over many units. So far, however, only four spacecraft using MMS parts have been constructed, resulting in little cost savings.

Yet another idea NASA has used to reduce costs is to employ the shuttle's unique capability to repair broken satellites and to return working ones to earth so that they could be refitted for a second mission. By developing a repair capability in space, NASA hoped to spend less on ground testing. By also reusing satellites, NASA hoped to get two missions for the price of one spacecraft. The shuttle's satellite repair capability has been used to rescue two disabled spacecraft to date, saving millions over what it would have cost to replace these satellites. Return and refitting has not been tried but is "on the books" for a late 1991 shuttle flight.

NEW STEPS
MUST BE TAKEN

As we have just seen, although several attempts to reduce costs have been tried, spacecraft costs remain high and are still increasing.

What measures could be taken in the future to lower satellite costs? One promising plan proposed by NASA is to buy relatively inexpensive communications satellites (which roll off assembly lines almost like tractors these days) and modify them for scientific missions! This will help alleviate the custom-assembly problem. The Mars observer mission will be the first to use a communications satellite.

What else could be done? Two ideas stand out. First, NASA must try to lower launch costs wherever possible. As we saw earlier, high launch costs drive up satellite costs. As described in Chapter Five, using expendable launch vehicles rather than the shuttle to deliver payloads to space, encouraging the start of a commercial launch industry, and developing the National Aero-Space Plane would each help achieve launch cost savings. As a further step, NASA could return to its old philosophy of building an extra satellite in each program, so that if one is lost during launch or because of a system failure, its backup could be used. Unused spare satellites could be converted for use on other missions for little additional cost. In this way, NASA could enjoy both a backup

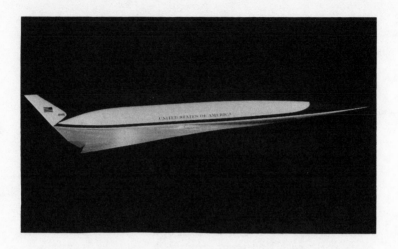

Pictured here is a model of one proposed design for the National Aero-Space Plane (NASP). NASP is intended to replace the shuttle by the year 2000 and make space transportation much less expensive.

capability and get a "two-for-one deal" on its projects. Just how useful such backups would be comes from testimony from the shuttle disaster. According to information given to the *Challenger* commission, an extra shuttle would have cost about $400 million to produce during the construction of *Challenger*, *Columbia*, *Discovery*, and *Atlantis*. Now, built on its own as a one-of-a-kind, the replacement for *Challenger* will cost over $2 billion!

If space is to become an important part of the national economy, the cost of building and operating satellites must come down. If NASA is to remain a viable national space agency, it must be able to conduct a variety of projects. The high cost of satellites is now threatening NASA's ability to do much more than operate the shuttle. Innovative ideas and the commitment to try them must be forthcoming.

C H A P T E R
E I G H T

THE FUTURE OF
THE SPACE PROGRAM

As we have seen throughout this book, the *Challenger* accident has created a new reality in the American space program. Although problems did exist in the pre-*Challenger* era, those problems seem small in comparison to the issues that confront the space program today. In almost every facet of space exploration and use, the destruction of the *Challenger* and its crew has had a major impact. The nearly simultaneous failure of two Titans and one Delta have also made their mark.

Since the shuttle and expendable rocket failures occurred in early 1986, many things have changed. NASA, for example, has been forced to examine every facet of the shuttle's design to search for weak points. The space station's design has also been reevaluated, and consideration is now being given to providing an escape vehicle for the station in case the shuttle fleet is grounded after the orbiting lab is manned. Also, launch insurance rates have increased dramatically (affecting many potential commercial efforts), and the once-strong U.S. space science program is in shambles.

The public's perception of NASA as a top-notch agency has been diminished. The *Challenger* and expendable rocket failures left the United States without a viable space transportation system. This, too, caused space commercialization efforts to be set back. Even the question of whether people belong in space at all is again under debate.

Had the shuttle disaster not happened, many things would be different. The Hubble Space Telescope would already be in orbit. The important Galileo mission to explore Jupiter and its moons would be under way, the spacecraft speeding its way across the solar system. With the shuttle flying, few people would have noticed the Delta, Atlas, and Titan failures, and some might even be saying, "It sure is a good thing we have the shuttle. Those old technology rockets aren't reliable—they needed phasing out." McDonnell Douglas's first materials processing plant in space would be producing drugs on the shuttle by now, and other space processing projects would be operating. Still, the shuttle disaster did happen, and the challenge facing policymakers and the public is to decide what kind of space program the United States will have for its future.

RECOVERY EFFORTS
GET UNDER WAY

It is expected that the shuttle program will resume flights in mid-1988. However, when the shuttle goes back into service, the number of its flights will be greatly reduced from original projections. This is primarily because NASA will have only three orbiters to fly all its missions until 1991, when a fourth will be ready. This reduced schedule has forced NASA to restructure its priorities for the use of the shuttle. Once flights resume, NASA plans to use the shuttle mostly for space construction, experimentation, military missions, and satellite repair. Most of the shuttle's satellite-launching work will be shifted to expendable rockets. Because of the increased budget crunch following the *Challenger* disaster, NASA is planning to fly many fewer scientific missions. (In fact, even those that aren't canceled may have to wait until 1990 or later to fly.) The agency may also have to scale back its plans for a permanently manned space station.

Concerning expendable launch vehicles, the sale of rockets by private industry has already begun. Martin Marietta's sale of a Titan 3 rocket in September 1986 to launch a Federal Express communications satellite marked the first such sale. Later that same month, the Delta launch vehicle got back on track from its earlier failure with a successful launch, and a weather satellite was successfully orbited by NASA on an Atlas booster. In January 1987, the air force decided to buy dozens of upgraded Delta ELVs to serve its needs and began to study a new Saturn-class heavy-lift launcher. By mid-1987, both the Martin Marietta Titan and the McDonnell Douglas Delta were each being readied for commercial launches.

Altogether, it seems the expendable rockets are going to have a strong comeback. It may even be that new-generation rockets like the Jarvis will be built to provide even greater launch capability.

A CRITICAL TIME

Even given the recovery efforts and successes of 1986 and early 1987, the space program is undergoing the most comprehensive overhaul and examination since its creation. Taking a pessimistic viewpoint, NASA today is smaller, more timid, more bureaucratic, and intellectually older than it was in the post-*Sputnik* era. And yet, in some ways the challenges are even greater than those it faced at the start of the Space Age thirty years ago.

In the late 1950s and early 1960s, there was broad agreement about our goals in space and a clear competitor: the Soviet Union. Since that time, both the goals and the competition have diffused. Today, the United States no longer dominates space. Instead, space is about evenly exploited by the Soviet Union, Europe, and the United States. Smaller efforts in China, Japan, and India are also proceeding. With huge federal deficits and a variety of social and military programs competing for funding, the space program faces a tough future. The period from 1988 to 1992 will be a particularly difficult one. During this period many things will have to go right. The shuttle must fly again with no major mishaps. The space station must be built, and space science must recover from its current ebb. A diverse private sector launch and space transportation system must arise and must prove itself reliable and economically competitive. Beyond these efforts, the space program must also set itself on a course for the future.

In 1986, four important national commissions made reports concerning the future course of the U.S. space program. The *Challenger* commission reported on how the shuttle program could recover. The National Academy of Sciences reported on the goals of space science for the period 1990–2000. NASA's Solar System Exploration Committee planned a vigorous program of planetary probes for the next twenty years. And, in the most wide-ranging report on space exploration since Apollo, President Reagan's National Commission on Space (the Paine Commission) set forth a plan for returning to the moon, sending people to Mars, and building a "space infrastructure" that would support space manufacturing and other economic endeavors.

A key thread running through the various debates in the recently released commission reports is the intimate tie between our future activities in space and the nation's economic future. Space technology clearly drives innovation as well as the development of new products and technologies on earth. As we have seen, space activities improve our international standing and contribute to full employment and a favorable balance of trade. Both President Reagan and Congress have endorsed the civilian space program as critical to the United States. Additionally, many believe that space-based military surveillance increases national security, and President Reagan believes that space-based defense could reduce or even "eliminate" the threat of nuclear war.

In the four-year period from 1988 to 1992, the United States must make a wide variety of decisions about how it will pursue its space program. If these decisions are poor ones, the United States may find itself in a situation much like that of 1957 and 1958— far behind other nations, trying desperately to catch up.

A SHORT-TERM PLAN
FOR RECOVERY

The most important short-term effort the United States must make in space is to get back into space. Once the United States reestablishes routine and reliable access to space with the shuttle and other vehicles, three key decisions must be made about the future of the space program.

First, policymakers must decide whether the United States wants to pursue a vigorous civilian space program. Since 1982, military space efforts have far exceeded those of NASA. Military requirements for communications, surveillance, and space defense satellites are great. However, it now appears that military payloads may fill the shuttle manifest, crowding out important scientific research and commercial payloads. Policy analysts, including John Logsdon of George Washington University and Richard Pike of the Federation of American Scientists, have noted that because the shuttle's primary user will be the military, it could be argued that a large part of NASA's budget is in fact going to support military activities. The first key decision the United States must make is to decide whether its future space program is to be primarily civilian or military.

The second key issue that must be faced in the next four years concerns the development of a space "infrastructure." Infrastructure is the supporting network of facilities and systems that makes routine activities possible. For example, the infrastructure of the United States includes its roads, bridges, and ports, as well as its communication and transportation networks. In space, only the bare bones of an infrastructure exist today. The present space infrastructure consists of the shuttle (as a transportation system) and the TDRS system network (tracking and data relay satellites). Probably the most important infrastructure items on the drawing board today are the space station and the National Aero-Space Plane. The Aero-Space Plane is a new generation shuttle that could cut the cost of space transportation by up to a factor of ten, thereby opening up whole new economic endeavors and scientific research avenues.

The final key decision that must be made concerns the type and level of scientific research that the nation feels it needs in the area of exploration and future space development. In addition to deciding how much to spend on research, policymakers must also decide which areas of research are most important. To date, most space research has focused on earth studies and astronomy. Over $25 billion has been spent sending probes to explore the planets, building and launching space observatories, and studying the atmosphere, oceans, and continents of the earth. Because the exploration of the planets may someday yield valuable mineral and other resources for us, this kind of exploration will almost certainly continue. However, other kinds of research may be more important to the economic development of space. Space medicine is one such area. If people are to live and work in space factories, the reaction of the human body to long-term weightlessness must be understood and techniques developed for the treatment of injuries such as burns, lacerations, and even acute illnesses in space.

Another area of the space program that has been neglected in the recent past is engineering technology. Since the late 1960s, very few new engineering projects have been funded by the government. In 1986, the NASA Advisory Commission called this situation critical and stated, "The nation has allowed its space technology base to erode, leaving it with little technological capability."[1] The development of new and better propulsion systems, a closed life-support system that would recycle wastes and produce food in space, and new power production systems are needed to spur economic and scientific development. Research into manufacturing processes, microgravity pharmaceutical production, and other "potential industrial applications" also need consideration.

These three issues—the importance of a civilian space effort, infrastructure development, and a new emphasis on research—must each be tackled if the U.S. space program is to have a vigorous future.

A LONG-TERM PLAN
FOR ECONOMIC STRENGTH

In the longer term, beyond 1991 or 1992, the United States must decide what its long-term goals in space are. In a recent report to the NASA administrator, the NASA Advisory Council stated that, "The nation has no long range goals [in space]," and that U.S. activities in space are neither "adequate nor sufficient [to retain] . . . U.S. preeminence."[2]

By contrast to U.S. space policy, both the Soviet and European space programs are well focused, with a clearly defined strategy for the future. Critics argue that much of the reason for NASA's lack of focus has been its "leashing" by successive administrations and Congress. As described in Chapter One, NASA announced in 1970 that it was prepared to build a space shuttle and a space station, send people to Mars, and conduct a vigorous program of unmanned exploration. Nearly twenty years later, the only element of this program that has been completed is the shuttle. The budget cuts and the scaling back of goals that were enforced on NASA since 1969 are directly to blame for this problem.

What kinds of long-term goals would stimulate the space program and return it to its once prominent position? Suggestions range from a lunar base and a manned Mars landing to a commitment to build inexpensive and reliable space transportation. The National Commission on Space has strongly urged that NASA develop a comprehensive space infrastructure and explore Mars with robots in the 1990s and then with people shortly after the turn of the century. Carl Sagan, an astronomer and president of the Planetary

The National Commission on Space has recommended that the United States set up bases on the moon and Mars. In this artist's rendering, a future Martian base is depicted.

Society, has lobbied for *international* exploration of Mars. Dr. Sagan says that this project could build better relations between the United States and the Soviet Union and spur technology. It has been estimated that setting up a Mars base could cost $100 billion, about what the Apollo effort cost in 1960s dollars.

Another proposal for a major new initiative is called the Global Geosciences program. This effort would focus the total combined research talents of many nations on a complete study of the earth's oceans, landmasses, and atmosphere, with particular emphasis on the impact of humans on the environment. Other large international projects have been suggested as well.

Whatever long-term projects are undertaken to restore U.S. leadership in space must meet three basic criteria. They must enthuse and motivate the public, particularly school children. They must offer society long-term economic benefits. And they must also stretch our technology so that the quality of life on earth is improved. Looking back on the Apollo project, the space shuttle, and the early exploration of the planets by space probes, we find that each of these efforts met such goals.

Like the space exploration of the past, future space activities will, for some time to come, be largely a government activity. This is natural, since from history we learn that the governments of Spain, Portugal, and Britain funded explorations of the New World, and the United States funded Lewis and Clark. Following these tax-supported government expeditions, settlers and tradespeople followed. If space is to be explored, settled, and industrialized, commitments must be made to spend public funds on it.

We do not know today the pace at which space industrialization and exploration will take place. This is something we must decide.

N O T E S

CHAPTER ONE

[1]Frederick C. Durant, ed., *Between Sputnik and the Shuttle: New Perspectives on American Astronautics*, American Astronautical Society History Series, Vol. 3 (San Diego: Univelt, Inc., 1981), 19.
[2] Ibid.
[3]John Noble Wilford, *We Reach the Moon* (New York: Bantam Books, 1969), 1.
[4]Dr. Thomas Kronke, in personal interview with author 22 May 1982 in Denver, CO.
[5]Durant, 68.
[6]Wilford, 269.
[7]Wilford, 101.
[8]John Logsdon, "The Space Shuttle Program: A Policy Failure," *Science*, Vol. 231, 30 May 1986, 1099.

CHAPTER TWO

[1]*Report of the Presidential Commission on the Space Shuttle Challenger Accident* (Government Printing Office, Washington, D.C.) 6 June 1986, 40.
[2]Ibid., 104.
[3]Ibid.
[4]Ibid.
[5]Ibid.
[6]Ibid., 198–201.
[7]Ibid.
[8]Ibid.
[9]"Leadership in Space: Yes or No?" *Aerospace America*, October 1986, 8–9.

CHAPTER THREE

[1]NASA-EP-123, *Why Man Explores*, 1976, 36.
[2]Edward B. Lindaman, *Space: A New Direction for Mankind* (New York: Harper & Row, 1969), 24.
[3]Dr. John Logsdon, in personal interview with author 28 May 1986 in Washington, D.C.

CHAPTER FOUR

[1]President's Message, *Space World*, March 1986, 40.
[2]Dr. Harlan Smith, in personal interview with author 4 Feb 1986 in Austin, TX.

CHAPTER FIVE

[1]Dr. Neil Hosenball, in personal interview with author 22 March 1986 in Boulder, CO.
[2]S. Payne and L. Colczak, "The White House Is Giving Business a Boost Into Space," *Business Week*, 25 Aug 1986, 43.
[3]"Starship 'Free Enterprise,' " *Newsweek*, 17 Sept 1984, 62.
[4]Ibid.
[5]Wolfgang Demisch, "You Can't Start Small and Grow," 74.
[6]David C. Scott, "Payoffs From Payloads: Brokers Scanning the Space Frontier," *The Christian Science Monitor*, 2 Oct 1984.

CHAPTER EIGHT

[1]"Advisory Group Questions NASA's Leadership Ability," *Aviation Week & Space Technology*, 26 Aug 1986, 26.
[2]Ibid.

FOR FURTHER READING

Clarke, A.C. *The Promise of Space*. Pyramid. New York, N.Y., 1970.

Durant, F.C., ed. *Between Sputnik and the Shuttle*. American Astronautical Society History Series. San Diego, Cal., 1981.

Finch, E.R., and A.L. Moore. *Astrobusiness*. Praeger Special Studies. New York, N.Y., 1985.

Lindaman, E. B. *Space: A New Direction for Mankind*. Harper and Row. New York, N.Y., 1969.

NASA EP-79. *Historical Sketch of NASA*. U.S. Government Printing Office. Washington, D.C., 1965.

NASA EP-123. *Why Man Explores*. U.S. Government Printing Office. Washington, D.C., 1976.

Oberg, J.E. *Red Star in Orbit*. Random House. New York, N.Y., 1981.

Pioneering the Space Frontier. The Report of the National Commission on Space. Bantam Books. New York, N.Y., 1986.

Poynter, M., and A. Lane. *Voyager, The Story of a Space Mission*. Atheneum. New York, N.Y., 1981.

Report of the Presidential Commission on the Space Shuttle Challenger Accident. U.S. Government Printing Office. Washington, D.C., 1986.

Riabchikov, E. *Russians in Space*. Doubleday. Garden City, N.Y., 1971.

Simpson, T.R., ed. *The Space Station*. IEEE Press. New York, N.Y., 1985.

Trento, Joseph J. *Prescription for Disaster from the Glory of Apollo to the Betrayal of the Shuttle*. Crown Publishers, Inc. New York, N.Y., 1987.

I N D E X